The High Weald
A Second Selection
IN OLD PHOTOGRAPHS

Yeomans Farm, Wadhurst, seen at the turn of the century when owned by Joe Field.

The High Weald
A Second Selection
IN OLD PHOTOGRAPHS

Collected by BRIAN HARWOOD

Alan Sutton Publishing Limited
Phoenix Mill · Far Thrupp
Stroud · Gloucestershire

British Library Cataloguing
in Publication Data

Harwood, Brian
 High Weald in Old Photographs
 Second Selection
 I. Title
 942.251

ISBN 0 7509 0334 1

Typeset in 9/10 Sabon.
Typesetting and origination by
Alan Sutton Publishing Limited.
Printed in Great Britain by
Redwood Books, Trowbridge.

First published 1993

Front cover illustration: Three fine working horses (and men) about to set off for another load of hay, probably on Edwin Beech's farm at Lamberhurst, *c.* 1905. The thatching of the stack roof seen behind appears in detail on page 14. (Courtesy Lamberhurst Local History Society)

Introduction

This photographic survey takes the reader into parts of the High Weald remaining from the first volume, and looks again at previously visited villages, only from new perspectives. No specific route is followed; instead the reader is allowed to meander through the lanes, woods and villages just as he might on a real life tour. The unexpected is often encountered with a turn of the page, exactly as might happen at a sharp bend in a remote lane.

Some of the old Anderida Forest still persists in the depicted localities. It was once 120 miles long east to west, and 30 miles across, and successfully kept invaders away from London. The Romans had to come across north Kent; the Normans created the Rapes of Sussex – coast to capital safe transit routes, each the responsibility of a Norman lord to keep open. The locals were largely left to live in their difficult and remote county as best they could.

First-time visitors passing through the Weald have left graphic accounts of their experiences – some are included in this volume – the paucity of intercommunicating routes having passed into Sussex folklore. Other, more recent travellers give more illuminating vignettes of the places that attracted their attention. For instance, while compiling his 1780 guide to the Tunbridge Wells locality, John Sprange visited some of the places in this volume. He found Bayham Place 'a very neat house', while Court Lodge at Lamberhurst was 'a most delightful spot'. Moving on to Frant, 'here is an exceeding good inn with rooms fitted up for the reception of genteel company'. Mayfield, he found, 'wears the pleasing appearance of plenty'. Touring back through Lamberhurst he commented, 'the town is only remarkable for being the great thoroughfare to Rye and Hastings', while Ticehurst was 'a small, ancient built village in which there is nothing curious or remarkable to entertain a stranger with'. All he could find to say about Wadhurst was, 'this place was once inhabited by a great number of Baptists'!

In the next century another traveller cast a much more analytical eye over the High Weald and, thankfully, left to posterity the fruits of his observations. He was William Courthope (1807–66), a lawyer and Somerset Herald at the College of Arms. Described by his contemporaries as 'the most accomplished historical Herald in the College', Courthope wrote an exhaustive study of every aspect of life and of family history, mainly in the localities of Wadhurst and Mayfield, but spilling over to most of the significant east Sussex villages and towns.

His survey is preserved in some forty-five copperplate volumes (Nos 16–61) kept at the college, covering, in brief, manorial, church, and general histories of both Mayfield and Wadhurst; volumes of family pedigrees for both towns, watercolours, line drawings, maps, engraved portraits, tricked arms, etc., etc., all covering the extent of the Loxfield Half Hundred; numerous parish register transcriptions, diaries of local travels and visits, and so on, and so on. Of quite exceptional and unique value to local historians of the Weald, the collection has lain at the college since Courthope's death in 1866, and only in the last decade has started to see again the light of day. The eight volumes covering Wadhurst and Mayfield parishes are now available for study on microfilm in the East Sussex Record Office at Lewes.

Another collection, not of a visitor, but of a resident, which perhaps deserves wider appreciation for its beauty as a record of contemporary Sussex life, exists at Lamberhurst. In this book the reader will learn something of the life of Henry Burrows; he left to the village a unique collection of photographic glass slides, detailing many and varied aspects of rural life on the Kent and Sussex border before and after the turn of the century. A man of diverse skills and artistic gifts, Henry Burrows' work deserves wider biographical appreciation.

Lastly, for Ticehurst, there exists the wonderful series of thousands of newspaper cuttings in the old Beech House Press workbooks. Running from Victorian times well into the present century, these encapsulate all facets of Ticehurst's daily business. The exploratory local historian counts himself highly lucky to come across just one collection of the types described above; in having been able to work from three, this compiler has found himself uniquely fortunate.

As Ian Keil said recently in *Local History*: 'Pictures make an immediate impact rarely possible for the written word.' The photograph may be a quick snapshot of a transient event, a deliberately posed group, a building or a rural scene. Finding a representative spread of such subject types is just part of the compiler's art; then follows the evaluation and interpretation. What is the subject? Not always as obvious as might appear, but a starting point that must be determined. Where was it? The location may prove to be the deciding interpretive factor. When was it pictured? This may be magnifying glass time! A minutely close study of dress, architectural detailing, vehicle types and the like can move a picture by twenty-five years each way. Why did the photograph get taken? A commercial reason? Family interest? All these factors come into the compiler's assessment when getting at the story behind the picture. But even given that all these parameters are in place, success does not always follow. One or two views stubbornly resist a clear interpretation of their content; at this point the compiler hands over to the reader and waits apprehensively by the letter box!

While it is hoped that an acceptable measure of success has been achieved in this compilation, the author claims no exhaustive knowledge of any of the subjects he has chosen to depict. He will, therefore, be only too happy to receive any advice or other information concerning detail accuracy from those better informed.

Brian Harwood

I will gather and carefully make my friends
Of the men of the Sussex Weald,
They watch the stars from silent folds,
They stiffly plough the field.
By them and the God of the South Country
My poor soul shall be healed.

If I ever become a rich man,
Or if ever I grow to be old,
I will build a house with deep thatch
To shelter me from the cold,
And there shall the Sussex songs be sung
And the story of Sussex told.

HILAIRE BELLOC, 'SUSSEX'

The visitor's first encounter with High Weald geography is generally along a lane such as this one at Witherenden, between Ticehurst and Burwash. Virtually unchanged today from this photograph of probably eighty years ago, it remains precipitously steep, serpentine, and high hedged. 'Narrow roads' such as this are copiously signposted throughout east Sussex. Not a few lead nowhere, petering out deep in the woods.

Travelling into the High Weald, it will not be long before the visitor happens upon local woodmen husbanding the forested land, just as they and their forebears have done these past twenty centuries. The depicted team are typical representatives although, unfortunately, their identities remain unknown.

An all too common occurrence on the infamous Sussex lanes, where subsidence always was (and continues to be) an occupational hazard for drivers. This one occurred in 1910 at Best Beach, Wadhurst, and took a total of 982 bags of cement (in 2 cwt bags) to repair. Looking on are Frank Goldsmith (with cycle), Kate Smith (with pram), and, in the slip, Charlie Baldwin, Harold Wright, Percy Newington and Will Mitten.

Charles Tompsett atop the hay wain at Yeomans Farm, Wadhurst, just before the First World War. Mr Tompsett was bandmaster of the Wadhurst Town Band for many years; he was heard across the nation in 1950 when he was one of the six contestants in the visiting 'Have a Go' radio programme.

The first owner of a motor car in the village of Hurst Green, William Hartnup, proudly sets off in his auto which might be a Buick of *c.* 1912 but perhaps owes more to the 'Bitsa' marque.

A game shoot at Court Lodge Estate, Lamberhurst, in 1907. The youngster in the centre with the armband is probably a member of the Morland family, the owners of Court Lodge.

Lower High Street, Wadhurst, at the turn of the century. On the left is the old frontage of the paygate cottage where, for some eighty years, the village shoe-mending business was run by Millie Reed (below) and her father.

A well known character in Wadhurst for many years, Amelia ('Milly') Reed ran her shoe-mending business from the old paygate cottage in Lower High Street. She took it over from her father, Charlie, in the 1920s and continued successfully until the 1960s. The photograph shows her in around 1938. The boot-patching machine shown had probably existed since the start of the business; even the Singer Sewing Machine Company is unable to say how old it is. Charlie Reed was involved with the football club for some fifty-four years and often helped out with kit repairs in his shop.

In many towns and villages across the country the occasion of Queen Victoria's Jubilee in 1897 was marked by the erection and dedication of shopping parades and housing schemes. Thus today a generous number of 'Jubilee Cottages', 'Victoria Parades' and the like still survives. Here we see Lamberhurst's contribution to the genre, Victoria House, pictured in the early 1900s. For centuries before this development the medieval Redd Lion Inn stood on the site.

The old Tollgate Cottage at Ladymeads Corner near Cousley Wood, seen in the 1890s. It was demolished in 1901. The large white boards on the cottage wall list toll charges payable by passing transport.

Another tollgate cottage, this time at Hurst Green, pictured before 1892 when it was demolished to make way for the old Court House building. The latter still survives, although it has not fulfilled its legal role for many years now. The premises have been converted to commercial use.

A spur of the moment photograph, taken in 1905, showing thatching on Edwin Beech's farm at Lamberhurst. The scene could be a guide for modern thatchers. On top of the ladder is Jimmy Willett, using a 'leggat' to pull into place a fresh bundle of thatch, a 'yealm'. His helper on the ladder holds ready a split hazel stick, a 'sway', used to tie down the yealms; the sways already in place form the dark line across the rick roof. The other man, by the rick, splits the hazel 'spars' into sways using a 'spar hook'.

A view into Frant, taken in the early 1900s, which it is almost impossible to imagine today; these houses are now perpetually divided by a noisy stream of traffic. Was it really once so peaceful?

The milk deliveryman of Burwash, known to everyone as 'Harold', plying his trade along the deserted village High Street in the 1930s.

Replacing oak shingles on the tower of Ticehurst church in 1949. Mr J. Walker (foreground) is helped by Mr R. Burnell. In the background is Romany Cottage, apparently ornately timbered but the wood is, in fact, just decorative paintwork. Today the cottage, re-roofed and without dormer windows, presents a smartly painted, unadorned brick frontage to Church Street. Abutting it on the right is Cinque Cottage which retains genuine timber framing infilled with plaster. Both cottages date from at least the seventeenth century.

The Middle House, Mayfield.

A fine example of real Tudor timbering. Viewed in the 1920s, the Middle House had stood in Mayfield since around 1575. From then to 1926 it was a private house, following which it became a widely known inn of high esteem. It continues so today.

Wardsbrook Farmhouse, between Ticehurst and Stonegate, is a rural version of timber construction, the main building dating from the early 1500s. Records date back, however, to 1372. Ownership can be traced to 1499, when William Saunders was the farmer. The steep roofs conceal the original 'queen post' construction.

Lamberhurst School originally opened in 1834, with a starting occupancy of fifty boys and fifty girls; it was enlarged the following year to take seventy boys. After a bequest in 1846 from local philanthropist W.A. Morland a second storey was added to the building together with the 'Dutch' style clocktower (above). Later expansion schemes transformed the upper floor from dormer to Dutch gable design, matching the tower and giving the school its present-day façade (left). The most influential schoolmaster of the Victorian era was F.S. Jeffrey (Headmaster from 1878 to 1900), who, in his first year there, found the children 'very ignorant and disorderly'. By the application of well tried methods, however, he had achieved notable scholastic advances a couple of years later, when the school inspectors reported a dramatic improvement in standards. Since then the school has never looked back. Mr Jeffrey, and some of his early charges, can be seen on page 155.

When cars really were cars! This Napier, pictured around 1910 at Lamberhurst, is being driven by George Bean, his son Alfred flying the red flag in front. The car's actual owner was Mr Simpson of Smith's Brewery. As he is said to have had the first car in the village, this is probably it.

The road leading south out of Hurst Green towards Robertsbridge via Silver Hill, long before the A21 was built. Even among Sussex roads this stretch had a malignant reputation. In 1752 Horace Walpole was unfortunate enough to travel it: 'Here our woes increased. The roads grew bad beyond all badness . . . however, without being all killed, we got down a famous precipice called Silver Hill and about ten arrived at a wretched village called Rotherbridge. Alas! There was only one bed to be had, all the rest were inhabited by smugglers.' Later, returning in daylight, Walpole saw from Silver Hill summit 'a whole horizon of the richest blue prospect you ever saw'.

The view across Ticehurst Square in the mid-1870s, long before the village well of 1888 was constructed and before the garden of Steellands, to the left, extended down to the road. Originally built by Henry Apsley in the 1690s, Steellands is known today as Apsley Court. To the centre of the view is the crown post roof of the fifteenth-century house called The Yett. Note the size of the barrels stacked by the wall of Mr Farley's forge, which were presumably manhandled into and out of the Duke of York's cellars.

Victorian Mark Cross schoolgirls playing hockey in the field opposite their school. This field also had a cricket pitch and was the venue for a very popular annual flower show. The land would be looked for in vain today; the heavily used A267 has replaced most of the grass.

Lamberhurst High Street in 1862, showing School Hill. The old bridge across the River Teise was formerly the old county border. Thus, we stand in Sussex and look over the bridge to Kent. Many sections of the Sussex county border have followed rivers; the more accurate placing of boundaries was almost impossible in the dense forests of Andredsweald until almost the 1800s. In 1895 a border realignment moved all of Lamberhurst out of Sussex and into Kent. On the right stands the Chequers Inn, which originated as a twelfth-century manor house and became an inn a century later.

William Horace Newington's old shop at Bayham Prospect, Station Road, Wadhurst, *c*. 1905. The Newingtons had an established grocery business at least as early as 1810, when records show that the founder, Joseph Newington, paid 1s. 10½d. for a year's rates.

The same property around five years later. The old crumbling stone frontage has been replaced with a smart railing and gate.

The business, post 1920. Connected to the phone and well established in a fine glazed showroom, W.H. Newington continued trading here for another fifty years, until the property was converted to a private residence in 1979. The smartly dressed proprietor proudly takes centre stage.

A group of carefree Edwardian belles and their beaux enjoying some sunshine, probably on the estate of Lord Courthope at Whiligh, between Ticehurst and Wadhurst.

Ticehurst National School in the 1880s. Built originally in 1846, the school replaced an 1830s two-roomed building in the nearby churchyard. Back in 1603 a 'scholemaster, Bartholomew Martindale', is recorded as living in the village but where, and what he taught, is not known.

Ticehurst girls pose for their school coronation photograph, July 1902. Back row, left to right: Kate Trinamer, Louise Preace, Isabel Balcombe, Minnie Lemmon, Olive Leaney, Mabel Eversfield, Alice Sibbald, Kate Young, Lettie Walters, Emma Roots. Middle row: Lilian Sheather, Mary Piper, Annie Baldwin, Ruth Leaney, Emily Baker, Alice Young, Flo Baldwin, Sis Sims. Seated: Kate Moren, Winnie Trimmer, May Baker, Daisy Winchester, Rose Young, -?-, Flo Leaney, Annie Sims, May Lemmon, Kate Baldwin, Violet Lemmon, Miss Covington. Half a century earlier some eighty-five girls and seventy-five boys, aged from 3 to 12, were being taught at Ticehurst. They had five weeks 'hopping' holiday, plus 'a few occasional days'.

Burwash schoolchildren ribbon dancing on the croquet lawn (at the vicarage?), *c.* 1910. The spinning wheel outside the summer house adds to the air of rural relaxation. Burwash still boasts one of the oldest village schools in the locality, it having existed since 1726. A school inspector's report of 1844 recorded that it had eighty-six boys and eighty-four girls aged between 6 and 12. They had five weeks harvest holiday, and one week at Christmas. Children of the poor were educated free, but those from farmers' and tradesmens' families paid 2s. 6d. a quarter.

The Greyhound Commercial Hotel at Wadhurst before 1888. The entrance to the market saleyard is on the right; after 1888 it was moved along the High Street, next to the old post office building. At this time the Greyhound's landlord was Jacob Pitt, a renowned cricketer, local administrator, and *bon viveur*. Although its recent history is documented back to the early 1800s, an inn known as 'The Grazehound' existed on the site in 1580.

Old Farm, Dale Hill, Ticehurst, *c.* 1937. The pond was filled in not long after. The tile-hung exterior conceals extensive timber framing dating the house back to the fifteenth century.

Jack Tompsett's old-established butchers business in Station Road, Hurst Green. He is shown to the right; the date is the mid-1930s.

An unidentified event attracting attention outside the Royal George Hotel at Hurst Green in the early 1900s. The cart seems to be arranged for some kind of display seating; details of what is going on are obviously being worked out at the bar of this old inn. The royal coat-of-arms over the portico of today's Royal George is in cast iron from the Hurst Green foundry (see page 69).

The Lamberhurst postal team in the early years of the century. Left to right: Messrs Duval, Gravett, C. Smith, B. Ladd, Lacock, C. Fayres, P. Harriss.

Tidebrook post office. On the road between Mayfield and Wadhurst, these premises are now Pennymill Cottage. The date is around 1910, when the Wallis family ran the business. The post used to be cycled to and from Wadhurst by George Wallis on his penny-farthing. After a brief interval at the house called Pine Lodge, the post office service to the village was shut down in 1968.

Young Cicely Bassett, photographed with her favourite doll at 4 Pilbeams Cottages, Faircrouch Road, Wadhurst. The date is 1896 and she is around three years old.

The Bassetts at Pilbeam Cottages in 1902. Young Cicely sits in the pony trap with her brother John ('Jack'), while her other brother, Thomas, holds the horse. Their father, Charles, holds the reins on Jenny, who is hitched to the trap he built in his coachbuilding business. Sir George Barham purchased Pilbeam Cottages in 1903 and renamed them Ingoldsby Cottages, recalling his Victorian relative's (Revd R.H. Barham) book *Ingoldsby Legends*.

Wadhurst schoolchildren dressed in blue sashes for maypole dancing, 1905. Cicely Bassett is behind Headmistress Hannah Watson, who was famous for never being seen without her hat. The event they probably took part in is shown on pages 36–7. At the time of writing Cicely Bassett is approaching 100 years old and living in Heathfield.

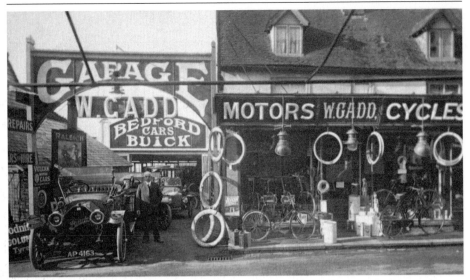

The motor trade takes root in Wadhurst (*c.* 1914) in the form of William Gadd's all-purpose car and cycle business in the High Street. The proprietor is seen standing by a handsome Buick, for which he was the local agent.

Charles Baldwin's rival motor agency at Durgates, *c.* 1907. Left to right: Dr C.H. Fazan and Frank Newington in the doctor's 6hp French steam car, Mr Corke with a Quadrant autocycle, Charles Baldwin astride an Enfield of around 1901. Frank Newington, then an apprentice at Baldwins, later claimed to have driven from 1903 to his retirement in 1973 without ever having an accident.

The Gurr family butchers shop in Lamberhurst, (*c.* 1906), pictured by local photographer Henry Burrows. The latter was one of the leading photography experts in the district and always composed his subjects with great care. Left to right: E. Gurr, S. Gurr, L. Gurr, Mrs W. Gurr, A. Gurr.

Court Lodge, Lamberhurst, at the turn of the century. Home of the Morland family since 1733, it is engulfed in rhododendrons and ivy. The glass façade to the side of the house (later a greenhouse) was originally a covered walk connecting the service end of the house with the family wing.

William Courtenay Morland MA (1818–1909). Popularly known as 'the old Squire', he lived at Court Lodge for some sixty-three years. At his death he was the oldest JP in Kent and Sussex, and the oldest parish council chairman in the country. A lifelong philanthropist, he founded Lamberhurst Working Men's Club in 1877 and the village children's Penny Bank, and was president and chairman of most village societies. A renowned farmer, he jointly grew most of the hops around Lamberhurst with E.W. Hussey, and his Court Lodge flock of Kent sheep won many prizes. In 1843 he married Margaret Cater, daughter of Gen. Sir William Cater; they had three children.

Probably the only time a Cavalier made an appearance in what was Parliamentarian Wadhurst. Behind the safety of an elapsed two-and-a-half centuries a Royalist (and friends) re-emerged for the peace celebrations of July 1919. The disguises conceal, left to right: E. Ballard, H. Boorman, F. Foot, F. Griffin, H. Austen.

The funeral cortège of George John Courthope arriving at Ticehurst, 10 September 1910. The mourners walked there from the Whiligh estate, a couple of miles away. Mr W.G. Foot is directing operations in the centre. Aged 61, Mr Courthope had had a distinguished career as an Inner Temple barrister. He was survived by three sons and three daughters, his wife Elinor having predeceased him in 1895. The car on the right is a Vauxhall, and the one in the centre probably an Alldays.

The Annual Fair in Wadhurst in the early 1900s, on 'Mr Cheesman's Field' behind the Institute. Thus Wadhurst folk used to exercise the Charter rights granted to them by Henry III in 1253, namely ' . . . a fair every year to last for three days, being on the Vigil,

the Day, and the Morrow of the feast of the Apostles Peter and Paul'. That is, the 28, 29 and 30 June. To the left, organizing her schoolgirls, is Headmistress Hannah Watson.

Laying the foundation stone of Chester Hall, Lamberhurst, 1906. That September the *Courier* wrote: 'Since the Brewery Hall has not been available owing to pressure of business, the inhabitants have been put to great inconvenience for the want of a central hall in the village. We are pleased to say the want will be met, as Mr E. Beech, of the Chequers Hotel, has decided to build a hall.' The new amenity lasted until the 1950s, when it was converted into a garage. (Mr Beech is pictured with his family on page 81.)

Old Jack Oyler, deliveryman of the Stone Cross Dairy Farm at Wadhurst. Pictured around 1910, he emigrated to Canada in 1912, married, and settled in Toronto, working for Canadian Timber Mills. Stone Cross Farm was run by Henry Edgar Boorman from 1911 until his death in 1924. It was then managed by his sons, Cecil and William, until their deaths in 1964.

Dunsters Mill, Ticehurst, in the 1920s. It had been working here since the 1400s, but in 1973, when approval was given for the flooding of the valley for the creation of the Bewl Bridge Reservoir dam, the building was moved some 500 yards, to above the waterline, at the expense of Southern Water Authority.

Frant Schools in their class uniforms at the turn of the century. Look closely at the school porch. Thinking he is unseen, one camera-shy urchin expresses his opinion with a hands-to-ears gesture. One wonders what retribution was exacted when the photograph was developed and circulated!

The Whapham family posing glumly for the camera (even the dog looks bored) at Homestalls, Five Ashes, *c.* 1892. Their names are mostly taken from the Bible. Standing, left to right: Eli, Lucy, Samuel, Ijon, Kerren-Happuch. Seated: Hephzibah, James, Elizabeth, Luther. Front row: Kezia, Jonathan.

Ijon Whapham, ploughing with Kitty, at Park Farm near Burwash in the 1920s.

Many a hay tedder now rusts, forgotten, in a farmyard corner. Here one is being worked with skill near Burwash in the 1930s by a smartly cap-and-jacketed Ronald Whapham. From the beautiful backdrop one can actually scent the lovely new-mown hay.

The traction engine driven thresher, a once universal harvesting machine. This one, owned by John Willett (with bike?) is being used near Owl's Castle Farm, Lamberhurst, in 1905. On its side is the main drive pulley, which took the belt drive from the traction engine. Very often these machines were seen in convoy: steam engine, thresher, straw elevator, and a wooden hut in which the team lived while away from their villages.

Lucy Whapham's wedding to Mr Hazelden at Horley Green, near Five Ashes, in 1912. The groom's brother is the Royal Marine just behind him. The photograph is owned by Doris Pagden (front row, second from left). Meanwhile, Doris Pagden's mother is seen grim-faced (back row, third from right). Her husband and his brother Eric (back row, sixth from right and third from left, respectively) would not forsake their cloth caps for the formality of wedding hats, so a fierce row ensued. This abated briefly as the camera call was arranged, with the participants putting as much distance between themselves as the camera would allow. Doris Pagden recalls that things heated up again soon afterwards!

All in their 'Sunday best'. Mr and Mrs Bellingham (far left and far right) and their guests prepare their donkey cart for a drive between Mark Cross and Rotherfield in the 1890s. Such domestic transport was as common then as the motor car today. Everybody knew how to assemble the harness, buckle and adjust it to the animal used, and correctly affix both to the cart. Most could also drive the combination along the winding Sussex lanes.

Keylands Cottage on Rudyard Kipling's estate, Batemans, at Burwash. The house was rented in the 1930s by agricultural author W.A. Ramsay, who wrote a series of anecdotes about Kipling and animals. Seen here at about the same date are some of Kipling's herd of red Sussex cattle. These he saw out of the window at Batemans when he penned the lines: 'And red beside wide-bankèd Ouse lie down our Sussex steers.'

The harsher side of the hop garden. Up to his shins in mire, James Whapham dunging-in the mounds at Park Farm, Burwash, around 1934.

In the distance, Rudyard Kipling's house, Batemans; in the foreground a plate on a pole. When the largest ship of its day, the *Queen Mary*, was launched on 26 September 1934, Kipling was so absorbed with the giant size of the vessel that he decided to pace out its length on his estate. He did this by walking in a straight line from his back door across the adjoining fields. Arriving at what he deduced to be the correct distance, he marked the spot with this platter-topped pole. If Kipling got his calculations right, the length of his walk should have been 1,019½ ft. The race for the biggest and best in the transatlantic liners was started by the French in 1932 with the launch of the *Normandie*. For a couple of years it was, at 1,029 ft, the first ship to exceed 1,000 ft in length; then came the *Queen Mary*.

A young Derek Warren (left) with his parents *c.* 1930, and (below) with the family dog some five years earlier. The widely esteemed Warren's Coach Company of Ticehurst was started by Derek's father Philip in 1919. When not helping out in Jack Dowling's village slaughterhouse, Derek started to learn the public carriage business. Warren's first transport was two Model T Ford vans which Mr and Mrs Warren drove (carrying anything) between Ticehurst and Tunbridge Wells. Enlisted into the forces, Derek was taken prisoner in Italy, but with bravery and an indomitable spirit he escaped in a lone trek over the Alps to Switzerland. His fortitude earned him the Military Medal and also a lifetime legacy of frostbite injury. He joined his father in 1946 to run the coach business, taking sole control on Philip's death in the 1960s. A determined and successful operator, Derek Warren took his village business across all the major European routes. He was also a valued parish councillor, outspoken and forthright on anything affecting his community. Indeed, it was his liking 'to call a spade a spade' that, in earlier years, led to frequent entries in the Village Institute Minute Books recording his being periodically 'banned' for 'unruliness'. Derek Warren died in 1989.

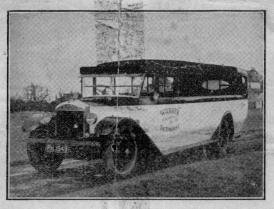
A typical Warrens timetable from the 1920s, competitively priced, and routed through all the major suburban commercial points. At this date horsed traffic was still a dominant feature of the London streets, many of which were paved with wooden blocks, set in pitch. The purpose of these 'setts' was to muffle the clangour of iron cart tyres on the road.

One of Warrens major rivals – AUTOCAR ('Pick up Anywhere') – at the Bell in Ticehurst in the 1920s. This was the period of almost suicidal fare and timetable wars, when opposing coach operators literally ran each other off the road, and raced from stop to stop to poach passengers. Fares fell to 3d., 2d., and 1d. a ride. The main protagonists, AUTOCAR and RED-CAR, eventually failed and were taken over by Maidstone & District in the mid-1930s. Warrens survived it all.

A Salvation Army outing in 1936, about to depart from St James's Square at Wadhurst, courtesy of Warrens Coaches.

St Alban's, Frant

The parish church of St Alban in the 1920s, about a century after its original construction. There had been an old church on the site for centuries before the Regency rebuild, certainly from medieval times, and a post-Domesday Chapel preceded that. The present lovely lychgate dates from 1964 and commemorates the dead of the First and Second World Wars, including a village VC, awarded to Lt. Christie Cookson in 1915. It leads on to a village churchyard quite unusual in the variety of its memorials connected to places, events and persons overseas. Principal among these is the monument to Colonel John By. Originally commissioned into the Royal Engineers, he was called from retirement in Frant in 1825 to go to Canada and build what became the Rideau Canal. The canal construction camp near the Ottawa River became known as Bytown. Colonel By returned to Frant in 1832, dying there four years later. Though his churchyard memorial is substantial, his Canadian one is continental in scale. Bytown grew into a prominent trading centre; in 1867 it was chosen as the new nation's capital, its name becoming Ottawa.

The very epitome of the prim and proper Victorian gentlewoman: Miss Anne Hankey (left), formerly of Frant, at Holly Bank, Dale Hill, Ticehurst, and together with her companion, Miss Batey (below). The eldest daughter of George Hankey JP, Miss Hankey left Frant to live at Dale Hill to be near her adopted work caring for the under privileged at Ticehurst Workhouse (see pages 144–5).

After Miss Hankey's death in February 1905 aged 61, it was written in the parish magazine, 'the Master and Matron and Chaplain of the Workhouse deeply lament the deprivation of an influence bright and loving, which made the inmates better and happier.' Miss Hankey was buried with her family at Frant, but a monumental cross to her was erected in Ticehurst churchyard by subscription. A new harmonium was also purchased for the workhouse chapel. Her sister Beatrice gave an address to the village in Ticehurst Institute, describing her sister's career.

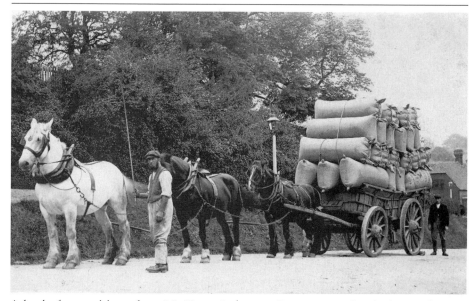

A load of pressed hops from Mr Hussey's farm at Scotney, near Lamberhurst, about to move off behind a massive Percheron lead horse. The stamped details just visible on the bottom rear hop pocket give the date as 1908. Such markings had to accord with the Hop (Prevention of Fraud) Act, 1866, which required details to be in letters 3 in high, and to include the grower's name, parish, county and year in which grown, and the progressive number of the pocket. Each pressed pocket weighed between 1½ and 1¾ cwt.

Green hops loosely packed in pokes, leaving a Lamberhurst hop garden in the early 1900s. They have just been picked.

The main road through Ticehurst, *c.* 1905. The site of Waterhouse's Stores to the left was originally occupied by the village Poor House and Charity School, established in 1761. This was made redundant by the erection of the Ticehurst Union Workhouse at Flimwell in 1835, which combined the care of eight adjoining parishes. By 1840 Mr Waterhouse had set up shop as depicted. The family continued in business there until the closure of the premises in the 1960s.

Ticehurst in 1904. The Bell Inn at the far end is a 'Commercial House', while The Unicorn (run by ex-smuggler Mr Tapley) stood at the point facing the man on the right. The tall, square building just past the butchers premises on the left housed Beech House Press for many years (see page 106).

Lamberhurst in the 1880s. A cat and, in the distance, one person seem to be the only animate objects disturbing the peace.

A game of marbles in Hurst Green High Street absorbs local youngsters in the early 1900s. Today the village post office occupies the premises to the right, but it was once one of those typical village shops selling every amenity from clothes to clothes pegs, all dispensed with copious helpings of local gossip.

Wadhurst agricultural gentry cast a critical gaze over a turn of the century ploughing match.

F.R. Gibb's coachbuilding, undertaking and carpentry business at the bottom of Best Beech Hill outside Wadhurst, *c.* 1910. Further along the row is George Gallup's forge. Today Gibb's premises are owned by W. Hodder, the builder.

Town Mill and Barn, Lamberhurst, in the 1870s. Town Mill has a history traceable back to before the Conquest as primarily a cider mill. In the 1400s a 'tippling house' existed on the site, known as 'The Vine'. It was further developed after its acquisition around 1487 by the Fowle family, ironmasters who, during the century of their occupancy, built the present Mill House. The mill changed from fruit milling to grist in the 1500s, which continued until its closure in 1910. It stood derelict for many years before its demolition in 1947. The renowned Lamberhurst photographer and artist Henry Burrows (see page 83) lived in part of Mill House and used a lean-to there as his studio.

Rehoboth Particular Baptist chapel at Pell Green, near Wadhurst, in 1938. At this date the chapel had stood for 114 years, being built in 1824 for the sum of £213 5s. 7d. Today it is suffering from a decade of neglect (though, at the time of writing, renewed efforts are being made to put it in better repair), but in its heyday it attracted up to 500 persons for services conducted by its founder, William Crouch. The notice seen above the door also explains that it was licensed for marriages. Well kept and well attended, the building was a feature of local interest until the 1950s, after which it declined.

Travelling hawkers at Lamberhurst, probably in 1911. The legend on the cart reads: 'Maria Gurr, License Hawker, Scouteyard, Lamberst, Kent.' A close look at the features of the family shows the deeply etched privations of their lifestyle. The horse, however, is well groomed, well shod and well fed.

The old Fountain Inn at Tidebrook, between Wadhurst and Mayfield, with Pennyfield Cottages adjoining to the left. The Fountain is documented back to 1860, when it was run by Charles Weston; it was in business for just a century, being closed in 1960. In the 1920s a notable social event was the Friday evening meet of the Fountain Inn Rat Club, 'tales of tails' being the order of the evening. During the Second World War, Miss Blaikley, writing in her 1942 diary *No Soldier*, mentioned that the cellar stairs of the Fountain offered a useful refuge in an air raid.

The Wesleyan church at Ticehurst was built in 1897, replacing earlier chapels of 1840 and 1821. Still there today, it now leads a new life as a private dwelling, following a period as business premises. Nonconformity had an early start in Ticehurst, namely 'at the house of Thankfull Hunt' in the year 1691 under the ministry of Jonathan Morton.

The Lake at the Marquess of Camden's estate at Bayham being cleared and deepened in 1897. Where the trucks of soil were transported to is not clear, but several steep-sided banks flanking the lake today may hide the answer. The original lake and the Water Garden were built in the late 1700s by the landscape gardener Humphrey Repton (1752–1818), but Camden family arguments meant that Repton's accompanying mansion was never built. The house visible today dates from 1872 and is by David Brandon. Bayham Lake is now a leading freshwater trout fishery, its sylvan setting probably making it the most beautiful of its kind in the country.

Ticehurst before 1900, on a card posted in 1910. The wildlife-sustaining, luxuriant growth of the hedgerows delights the eye in a way that modern, machine-cropped, 'short back and sides' hedge-cutting never can.

Eridge Castle, home of the Marquess of Abergavenny, in the early 1930s. This survivor of the 'Gothic Revival cum Picturesque' movement is attributed to the brother of the governess of the Abergavennys' children. Building took place in fits and starts from 1790 to 1830. Designed for external impact, the castle had an ill-lit and cavernous interior, which proved impossible to keep in habitable condition. Architect John Denman truncated most of the battlements in his 1938–9 rebuilding project; further radical contractions in 1958 produced the house, Eridge Park, which survives today.

Edwardian peace along Mayfield High Street in pre-motor car days. Walnut Tree House (immediate left) dates from the early 1500s and was probably one of Mayfield's original shops.

Colourful participants in the Lamberhurst Children's Union Fête, 12 June 1935. Above: the Marchioness of Camden judges the fancy dress. Below: the fête procession winds its way to the grounds of Court Lodge.

A fine display of Shire horsepower at Pond Meadow, Lamberhurst, in the 1920s. Harnesses glistening, brasses shining, coats gleaming, manes and socks washed and combed, the breeds appear to be a mixture of Clydesdales and Shires with, perhaps, a Suffolk (second left). Even after the calamitous loss of horses to the First World War there still remained over a million working on farms in 1918, according to the agricultural census for that year. However, with the onset of tractor power the total had declined to just over 50,000 by 1960. But in recent times there has been a clear resurgence in the utilization of horse power, both for working and leisure use, a fact underlined by the increase in membership to heavy horse societies. Oxen were the universal beasts of burden on English farms until the early 1700s, when the 'cart horse' breeds, with their less lumbering physiques, supplanted them. Sussex was probably the last county to retain oxen, using them to good purpose on its clayey soil until well into the present century (see page 152). Working horses were often a farm's most valuable asset and needed careful looking after; charms were sometimes hung on the harness to ward off sickness and evil. These charms survive today in the horse brasses and harness bells which liberally bedeck Shire horses.

St Peter's church, Stonegate, near Ticehurst, probably in the 1890s. Stonegate first had its own church in 1838, but subsidence caused severe structural faults and it was demolished in 1904. The existing church was built the following year at the expense of G. Courthope of Whiligh, son of the patron of the original church. The site was a strange place upon which to rebuild; the continually sodden subsoil meant that as many bricks went into the foundations of the present church as its above-ground structure.

A special occasion in late 1940. Perhaps to mark victory in the Battle of Britain, the old 'uns of Ticehurst gathered together boasting a combined total age of nearly 700 years. Back row, left to right: Revd O.A.S. Edwards (50), Mr Bishop jnr. (73), Tom Pierce (82), Mr Boot (70), Mr Booker (73). Front row: Mr Orange Lemmon (91), Mr Dowling (81), Mr Bishop (84), Tom Croft (83).

Jabez Smith (1818–1907), Postmaster to Wadhurst for some forty-eight years. Originally from Hailsham, he came to Wadhurst after leaving school at twelve to apprentice as a currier in Smiths Tannery at Prospect House (now The Lodge). He continued this trade until 1851, when he was appointed Postmaster. In this role he not only ran the post office, but also delivered all the letters, 'in a smock frock and an old silk hat' recalls Wadhurst historian Alfred Wace. Following his retirement in 1888, Jabez Smith lived in this bungalow, which he had built for himself.

The Walk, Wadhurst, in the 1920s. The Walk had existed for almost a century. It was created for the convenience of the passing public by Thomas Wace, who owned Hill House (behind the wall to the left). The grove of trees was a later adornment: the original planting was paid for by concerts, given by the then newly formed Wadhurst Town Band.

Witherenden Mill, before its demolition between the wars. Witherenden was one of the oldest surviving water-driven flour mills in the locality, dating from the fifteenth century at least.

The Bull Inn, tucked away at a crossing of lanes outside Ticehurst. The inn has always enjoyed a quietly remote existence. It has been there some 500 years, though the tile-hanging and brickwork are relatively modern, and conceal much original timber-framing. One of The Bull's attractions occurs each Boxing Day on the field behind, when the annual 'Soccby' match is played. The field has football goalposts at one end and rugby posts at the other; the game changes from soccer to rugby, and vice versa, each time the ball crosses the halfway line. A ball of indeterminate shape is used and, fortified by visits to the bar, a wonderful time is had by all. The game is an old tradition, first mentioned in the Parish Magazine in 1901: 'Boxing Day – in the morning, a pick-up game of football – Reds and Blues.'

The leafy calm of Burwash High Street, *c.* 1907. The High Street has a past steeped in smuggling. In September 1721 a party of Grenadiers intercepted a gang carrying 'running tackle' at one end of the village. One of the gang, a noted 'owler' named Jervis, 'fired his pistols and retired with his men to a wood'. The Grenadiers fired back and the pursuit continued, tit-for-tat, cross-country from Burwash to Nutley, where the gang was rounded up and committed to Horsham gaol. At the other end of Burwash High Street a stroll today in the churchyard of St Bartholomew's reveals tombstones carved with skulls and crossbones – the resting-places of smugglers.

Providence Chapel, adjoining a beer shop in Flimwell in the 1890s. The chapel had a long and faithful attendance, the local paper recording in May 1907 that an 'Anniversary Service was held . . . with morning, evening and afternoon services . . . tea was provided and a good number sat down to the excellent spread.' Unfortunately, details of which anniversary are not given, but a 'Mr Kemp of Biddenden' was the principal preacher. By the First World War, however, the retail beer premises had expanded to include the chapel, the new business trading as the Welcome Stranger Inn.

The Welcome Stranger shop with characteristic pentice roof. The latter still survives, supported by the same stout tree trunks. At present the property is a restaurant. Outside it in 1906 are, from left to right: -?-, -?-, Joseph, Florence and Joseph (jnr.) Pankhurst.

Flimwell village, looking towards Ticehurst, *c*. 1870. Standing in the road (far centre), is Harry Mepham, a water-carrier. Piped water was not available to many Wealden villages until after the First World War, hence the water-carrier was an important and often seen member of the village community, carrying from well to household.

The youngsters of Tidebrook School in 1936. Many of those depicted were in the school when a VI bomb exploded across the road from it on 4 August 1944. Strict safety training saw them all in the air raid shelters as the bomb approached, and no one was injured. The school (dating from 1859) was wrecked and never rebuilt. A plaque in Tidebrook church gives thanks for the children's safety. Back row, left to right: D. Ellis, J. Knight, C. Smitherman, ? Blackman, M. Knight, B. Bassett, E. Baldock, P. Griffin. Middle row: D. Warren, J. Lancaster, R. Ballard, A. Baldock, J. Sutton, -?- , J. Fairweather. Front row: -?-, G. Spicer, -?-, -?-, B. Eaton, G. Lancaster.

Notable Flimwell trader William Barfoot with his wife Eliza, in the 1890s. Their relative, Ray Barfoot, recalls that they operated a renowned bacon-smoking and -curing business in outbuildings behind the shop. The latter, still there today, also housed a busy bakery. William also ran a contract horse-hire business, two farms at Rosemary Lane and Sunnybrook, and engaged in housebuilding around Ticehurst.

A group by the respected Lamberhurst photographer Henry Burrows. Mostly members of the Avard family (Mrs Avard is on the extreme right), they are seen outside their bakery and confectionery business, which still exists today. The date is around 1905.

The foundry at Hurst Green. It traced its origin back to 1704, when the Wealden iron industry was still an industrial force, and was run by the Huntley and Pierson families. In the mid-1800s it was bought by Albert Oakley. The Oakleys carried on the engineering and foundry business right up to 1972, then selling the site to Messrs Harper & Eede. The entire works – Cupola Furnace, Foundry, Fitting and Turning Shop, Pattern Loft and Smithy – was literally a museum-piece and, as such, was re-erected at Chalk Pits Museum in Amberley through Harper & Eede's generosity. A lifelong foundryman, the late Bill Oakley recalled farmhands working the furnace blower in their time-off and being paid in beer, which they drank out of their boots!

Left: Captain Charles Lamb of the King's Revenue cutter *The Stag*; below: Miss Elizabeth Boys of Elford, Hawkhurst. Both are pictured in 1786. The captain loved the lady, but the lady's father made every effort to keep them apart. In a desperate effort to destroy the liaison, Miss Boys was exiled with just a servant to a remote farmhouse at Fairlight. But the lovers' meetings continued on Fairlight Cliffs, at a point named in consequence 'The Lovers Seat'. In 1786 they eloped to London and married at St Clement Danes; the bride was promptly disinherited and disowned by her irate father. The captain eventually settled with his wife at Higham House, Salehurst. He was obviously well connected in London, for these marriage portraits are by Day & Son, royal lithographers.

But why was the match so vehemently opposed by Miss Boys' father? In 1749 the ringleaders of the infamous Hawkhurst gang of smugglers, 'The Sea Cocks', were publicly executed, but this only temporarily checked the movement of illicit goods through the High Wealden woods. Other, cleverer, smugglers took over the lucrative trade, using more sophisticated methods well into Victorian times. Mr Boys' vindictive behaviour towards his daughter's wish to marry a law-abiding man, especially one in the Revenue, clearly seems to imply that he was up to his ears in a Hawkhurst-based smuggling business.

Looking across from Ticehurst to the nearby hamlet of Three Leg Cross, *c.* 1920. Listed in a 1769 survey as part of 'Town Borough', Three Leg Cross remains little changed today; it is just a scattering of houses on a muddy junction of lanes in the fields.

Tilling the alleys in a Wealden hop garden, *c.* 1900. The men are using a specialist narrow plough, a 'nidget'. The sign on the pole in the background says 'No Footpath'; there was once probably a right of way here, but it has disappeared since.

A Bayham shooting party in the 1880s. The heir to the Camden estate, Lord Charles Pratt, is front right. Bayham has been in the Camden family since its acquisition in 1714. The existing mansion dates from 1872. In 1961 the old abbey ruins on the estate, dating from around 1208, were entrusted to the nation.

An early view of Frant, probably in the 1920s. To the right is Spencer Delves, the bakers.

Sparrows Green near Wadhurst, *c.* 1912. Note the use made of flat projecting shop rooftops for floral displays and ornamental ironwork in this view, and in the photograph above.

A shooting party on the estate of Sir Henry Goldfinch near Castle Hill, in 1892. The gentleman (far right) is possibly Sir Henry, while James Whapham, the Head Keeper (fifth from left) holds a trap. For the connoisseur a varied selection of shotguns is on display.

TICEHURST UNION.

CENSUS, 1881.

POPULATION OF EACH PARISH, &c., FROM 1831 TO 1881 INCLUSIVE.

PARISHES.	Population. 1831.	Population. 1841.	Population. 1851.	Population. 1861.	Population. 1871.	Houses. Inhabited.	Houses. Uninhabited.	Houses. Building.	Population. Males.	Population. Females.	Totals. 1881.
TICEHURST......	2314	2464	2850	2758	2954	570	14	2	1443	1564	3007
WADHURST......	2256	2482	2802	2480	3191	632	33	2	1630	1586	3216
SALEHURST ...	2204	2099	2196	2014	2080	428	20	2	1113	1020	2133
FRANT	2071	2274	2447	2469	3263	616	27	2	1592	1889	3481
BURWASH	1966	2080	2227	2142	2232	472	27	...	1151	1134	2285
LAMBERHURST	1521	1570	1734	1605	1812	376	15	...	901	965	1866
ETCHINGHAM...	686	812	950	864	894	180	16	2	466	441	907
BODIAM	349	377	306	303	306	63	6	...	161	163	324

The 1881 Ticehurst Union Census gave comparative totals for previous decades. The 1831 census only recorded numbers of persons; in 1841 names were recorded for the first time. In 1851 ages, birthplaces, marital status and relationships were added, and a church congregation survey was also carried out. Aliens were included in 1861, while in 1871 an attempt was made to count British persons across the Empire.

The striking timber construction called The Stage on top of Silver Hill, Hurst Green, 1927. Its lookout function was related to a Napoleonic field barracks nearby, set out around 1800 as part of the invasion defences. The Stage has long been demolished, but Stage Field was given to Hurst Green in 1949 to commemorate the Battle of Britain by the late Col. Hornblower of Etchingham. Horace Walpole enjoyed the view from here in 1752 (see page 19).

Looking down on Lamberhurst in 1929. The sun is high, the day half done – but where is the traffic? The old narrow bridge is still in place, slowing vehicle movement and helping to maintain a peaceful pace of life in the village.

Woodbine House in Ticehurst, with woodbine and two ladies of the Gillham family, *c.* 1900. The little low roof to the extreme right housed the first Ticehurst post office. In March 1902 'a telephonic system' was also established 'at Mr Gillhams'. Said a local correspondent, 'from the wires radiating from Mr Gillhams, you could almost imagine yourself in Cornhill'.

A society wedding at Eridge, 30 September 1884. The happy couple are Lady Alice Nevill and Captain H.C. Morland of Court Lodge, Lamberhurst. A local reporter filled 960 lines with admiring detail, but thought 'the organ was well out of tune'. His criticism hit a nerve and by 1891 a wonderful new French instrument by August Gern was installed in Frant church.

Outside 11 Church Street, Ticehurst, *c.* 1946. The group represents some of the oldest established village families. Back row, left to right: Nancy Gillham, Margery Vidler. Middle row: Violet Gillham, Minnie Lemmon. Front row: May Lemmon, Audrey Vidler, Mr Orange Lemmon. The latter was a long-serving and much respected manager of Coopers Stores.

West Street, Mayfield, *c.* 1905. The old man in the foreground may be wearing a smock from the smockery near the white building, visible just above the vehicle in the road.

An impressive arrival. Arthur Prudence, landlord of the Duke of York, Ticehurst, from 1927 to 1936, in his king-sized Renault. The Duke of York and The Bell alternated as venues for the annual Farmers' and Tradesmens' Dinner. In 1889 the Duke of York had the Toast 'Trade and Agriculture'. Mr Corke, responding for Trade, saw 'gleams of a brighter prospect', but Mr Manwaring, for Agriculture, 'doubted an improvement observable'. During the evening 'some glees by Mr T. Field's company separated the speeches'.

The Beech family, owners of the Chequers Inn at Lamberhurst, *c.* 1900.

A nondescript dwelling in the Cousley Wood fields *c.* 1906. It had achieved notoriety on 11 December 1905 when the resident, Mrs Frances Stevens, was murdered there by her son. With typical Edwardian vigour no detail was spared of the inquest's proceedings at the nearby Balaklava Inn. Descriptions abound of 'ghastly gaping wounds' and 'life blood gushing with great force to splash on the walls'. James Stevens was convicted of wilful murder at Lewes Assizes and sentenced to penal servitude for life, the evidence being insufficient for hanging. Called Pook Pit Cottage, the house stood at the junction of Whitegates Lane and Woods Green Road, formerly called Lambkin Corner.

The old Flimwell Stores run by the Pankhurst family, pictured *c.* 1890. At the door are, left to right: Joseph, Will and Elizabeth Pankhurst. The carrier is bringing flour from Kemps of Robertsbridge in a typical waterproof, tilt-covered wagon used for dry goods transport.

A junior Frank Packenham (later Lord Longford) leading the quarter-staff drill with the Hurst Green Boy Scouts, 1910.

Avuncular Henry Burrows of Lamberhurst, *c.* 1930, with Lady. Originally from Broadway in Worcestershire, he arrived at Lamberhurst in 1878 to be schoolmaster, pianist and organist. A man of many talents, he had spent his early years in show business as a member of the widely known Black Star Minstrel Troupe, touring Victorian music halls. His teaching career in Lamberhurst tended more towards the artistic than the academic, but his popularity kept him in his post for seventeen years. There then followed a notable career in photography, during which time a fascinating range of Lamberhurst subjects was depicted. Mr Burrows had a studio at Mill House (see page 55). After the First World War he taught until his retirement in 1927. As church organist he spent some fifty-seven years playing at the console of the old Bishop & Sons instrument.

Several generations of the Gurr family of Lamberhurst, depicted by Henry Burrows in 1910. The title: 'Following in Father's Footsteps.'

A Coffee Circle is the theme of this Henry Burrows montage for Easter Monday, 1908. The participants are unknown.

This cribbage school, photographed by Henry Burrows, is undated. The headgear may, however, offer a clue. The men on the right are wearing blue slouch hats of the Boers, adopted by the 1st Cinque Ports Rifle Volunteer Corps in 1902 after their campaigns with the Royal Sussex Regiment in the South African War. The uniform was discontinued in 1907 with the advent of new TA volunteer regiments. The man in the centre is wearing an old shako, which the slouch hat superseded. Perhaps the men are old soldiers reverting to type for the camera.

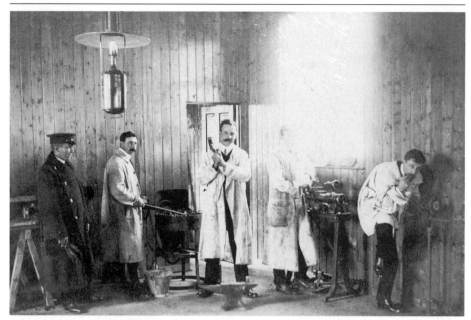

Henry Burrows entitled this scene for Easter Monday 1911 'A Busy Day'. Manual trades are shown, but why the soldier?

Lamberhurst Choir in the 1920s. Their musical skills owed much to the tuition of Henry Burrows, their organist for fifty-seven years. The high standard continues today in the form of the Lamberhurst (& District) Choral Society. Back row, left to right: W. Males, W. Crump, Miss D. Crump, L. Dean, Revd Jose, R. Milton, Mrs Green, B. Bones, A. Barham. Centre row: Mrs Crump, Mrs Dean. Front row: F. Bedley, M. Foster, R. Young, R. Playfoot, C. Manktelow, W. Simon, W. Wiglie, J. Bassett.

Sgt. Walter Vidler of Ticehurst in early 1900, prior to leaving for the South African War. He had enlisted into the Royal Sussex Regiment for active service from the 1st Cinque Ports Rifle Volunteer Corps; the latter covered all of Kent and East Sussex, their volunteers forming part of Kipling's 'fifty thousand horse and foot off to Table Bay'. Some of the experiences of soldiers from villages in this volume are given overleaf.

The spick and span Sergeants of 'C' Company, 1st Cinque Ports Rifle Volunteer Corps from Ticehurst (above) and their counterparts from Lamberhurst (right). The Ticehurst men are known but those from Lamberhurst are not. Standing (above), left to right: W. Mitten, W.J. Vidler, A.N. Jarvis, R.C. Morris. Front row: A. Stevenson, J.G. Tinto, T.P. Field. A remarkable collection of letters home from Walter Vidler survives in Ticehurst parish magazine. They were printed verbatim by Revd Arthur Eden. Vidler speaks about many other actions involving regiments with Cinque Ports Volunteers, so some of the men from Lamberhurst may well have been alongside him in battle. In March 1900 Vidler, Jarvis and Pte. Pilcher were 'dined out' of Ticehurst at the Duke of York before their embarkation. Afterwards the company moved on to the Institute, where 'proceedings were of a most enthusiastic character!' Ticehurst football captain William Pilbeam had already been drafted into the Rifle Brigade and preceded his fellow villagers to the Cape. Present at the Relief of Ladysmith, he described his food as hard biscuit, which he had to break with a stone, and corned beef. Water was 'very scarce' and there was 'nothing to wash in for four days'. Soon after he was wounded at the Battle of Colenso, where he saw 'shot and shell flying about in all directions'. He finally had a wash after twelve days.

Walter Vidler started his war in the wrong place: '. . . they took us to Durban by mistake and we stopped there a week.' He soon found the action, heading for Pretoria 'doing one of [Lord] Roberts' forced marches, about twenty miles a day, and laying out of a night with your overcoat and a blanket.' By September 1900 Sgt. Vidler had survived seven major battles, William Pilbeam had lost an eye, and both were invalided from the front with fevers. By implication all members of the RVC (some 320 men) suffered similarly; many in other units were killed. The Ticehurst men came home in June 1901 to a rapturous reception in the Duke of York. At a sit-down dinner, over fifty persons enjoyed an evening of fine food and songs. William Pilbeam's taste for adventure led him into more trouble in 1925, when he facilitated the escape of an Egyptian prince from Ticehurst House Mental Hospital. The prince returned to Egypt, but Pilbeam was arrested.

Enthusiastic pre-war members of Lamberhurst Church Lads Brigade. Back row, left to right: D. Fuller, K. Bish, R. Wallis, L. Perryman, J. Campany. Front row: D. Bassett, Revd E. Salisbury Jose, J. Dale. Not only Vicar of Lamberhurst for twenty-one years, but also Provincial Grand Chaplain of Kent, the Revd Jose had many skills. Born in Australia, he brought typical antipodean enthusiasm to his various extra-Vicarial activities. Eight times Captain of Lamberhurst Golf Club, he also played a competitive game of cricket. A leading Freemason, he came to occupy senior positions in the major Kent lodges. Revd Jose died at Hook Green in 1948 aged 74.

The people of Ticehurst collect together in their village square on 2 June 1902 to hear news of the ceasefire in the South African War. Revd Arthur Eden is reading the official despatch.

Summerhill Cottages, between Wallcrouch and Ticehurst, before (above) and after (below) a flying bomb attack in 1944. To some extent the tile-hung walls absorbed the blast, protecting the inner brickwork from more serious damage.

The dedication of the Ticehurst Second World War Memorial, 27 July 1947. Officiating is the Dean of Battle, Very Revd A.T.A. Naylor, assisted by the Vicar of Ticehurst, Revd O.A.S. Edwards.

The First World War Memorial dedication in Ticehurst Square, November 1923. The majority of men whose names are remembered on such monuments in Sussex fell on 9 May 1915. On that dreadful day the Royal Sussex Regiment was cut to pieces in the futile action at Aubers Ridge. Whole village families – sons, fathers, brothers – were wiped out in hours. Cooper's Stores employed twenty men before the First World War; eleven of them were killed. The brass plaque bearing their names affixed to the shop wall has been diligently polished from that day to this. Each Remembrance Day at Ticehurst the names of all the fallen are read out, one by one.

Ticehurst Royal British Legion members, just after the First World War. The British Legion started in Ticehurst on 25 June 1921, and since then their headquarters have been at The Bell Inn; thirty years later a woman's section was formed.

The sumptuous décor of the Museum, formerly in Ticehurst House, seen about 1891. Its surroundings were characteristic of all the rooms of the house. In its interior design, some Regency, some early Victorian, Ticehurst House was quite unique, and deserving of modern architectural study. Surviving drawings made by architect John Montier in 1827 show a remarkable range of facilities for the care of the mentally ill. The drawings can be seen today in the Wellcome Museum.

Ticehurst House chapel in early 1891, following 'remarkable improvements lately at the hands of the Drs Newington,' according to the parish magazine. Coloured walls, mosaic reredos set in carved oak, choristers' stalls and a pulpit, all in oak, as well as a stained glass window memorial to earlier doctors of the Newington family, and a new organ, all combined to create a wonderful focus of worship for staff and patients. None of it has survived later renovations.

A patient enjoys the unhurried pace of a donkey-drawn Bath chair in the peaceful groves around Ticehurst House, in the 1890s. In the grounds at this date some of the unique, exotic Regency garden buildings could still be seen – the Hermitage Pavilion; Gothic, Baroque, and Indian Summer Houses; the Moss House; the Pagoda; Italian Gardens, and a gold and silver Pheasant Aviary.

The Hare and Hounds crossroads at Flimwell, c. 1900. In the distance, the peace and quiet allows a horse to amble by itself across the road to graze, while its owners gather in conversation opposite.

Waiting for some traffic, a lone AA man takes centre stage at the Hawkhurst junction on the London to Hastings Road (the modern A21) in the early 1920s. The locality is virtually unchanged from that depicted on page 67.

The AA patrolman on traffic control in 1931. By the 1930s the inexorable growth of motorized traffic had led to the need to re-design the crossroads. Here the contractors move excavated soil across the road in railed trucks. The AA man's duty box used to be located opposite The Hare and Hounds, exactly where the gritting box now stands.

The Hare and Hounds at Flimwell, in its heyday between the Wars. Landlord A.E. Thatcher (pictured) sold oatmeal stout at 2s. 6d. for a dozen bottles, and 'Good Accomodation for Cyclists' was always available. Today the inn is closed and somewhat derelict, but cyclists are still plentiful on this scenic riding route. Perhaps one day this picturesque old inn will again participate in their pleasure.

Down on the farm at Bernhurst, Hurst Green; *c.* 1909. The infant Lord Longford makes friends with a carthorse.

Carnival Day in Burwash High Street, August 1932. Atop the penny-farthings are (left) Albert Richardson and Charles Pagden. A notable radio and stage entertainer, Albert 'Laddie' Richardson found national fame in 1929 due to his unique farmyard songs, which he performed with inimitable agricultural 'noises off'. Born in Burwash in 1905, he toured with various major entertainers (Laurel and Hardy, Flanagan and Allen) in England and Europe. On becoming Sexton of Burwash church he was promptly dubbed 'The Singing Sexton'. Joking and singing to the end, he died at home in Burwash in 1976.

An Edwardian view of Ticehurst village. Opinions vary as to the make of the motorcycle, a two-stroke, with round tank, belt drive, and outside flywheel on the off-side.

Old shop fronts along Wadhurst High Street in the 1890s. Most have that Wealden characteristic, an iron pentice. The people at the extreme left are standing outside the White Hart pub in its original siting. Ansell's long established business on the right continued for twenty years after the death of the owner in 1947 before being sold.

Mark Cross Mill in the 1880s. It had been operating continuously since 1760, a date when most tower mills of this type were first developed. The typical all-weather delivery cart can be seen in greater detail on page 82. In this view the component parts of the mill's 'fantail', the sail directional control mechanism, are clearly visible. When the sail-braking gear was released, the domed top could rotate into the wind.

Mark Cross Mill on fire during the night in 1911, a photograph taken by the vicar's daughter. After the fire the mill was rebuilt and operated intermittently until the Second World War. In 1960 it was converted into a private dwelling.

The debris after the fire. Some of the principal working parts of a typical tower mill are visible. Bottom left: the main spur wheel, providing the direct drive to (usually) three millstone sets. Front: the massive one-piece driving spar, which connected the sail drive to the spur wheel. Left: the two men are pulling out part of the iron worm which took the drive from the sails to the spar. Centre: millstone sets and brake wheel mechanism parts.

The all-conquering Flimwell footballers, depicted at the summit of their achievements in 1930. They had just won both the Weald of Kent League and the Ticehurst League. Mainstays of the team were, without question, the four Barfoot brothers (below). Alf alone amassed over a dozen winners' medals. Back row (above), left to right: H. Smith, R. Pantrey, A. Turner, F. Bailey, F. Pantrey, F. Colvin, W. Button. Middle row: J. Smithers, Arthur Barfoot, J. Dennis. Front row: W. Puxty, Fred Barfoot, Alf Barfoot, A. Barratt, Stan Barfoot.

Left to right: Stan, Fred, Alf, and Arthur Barfoot. Their Flimwell football team won the Weald of Kent League in 1927, 1928, 1929 and 1930, and also the Ticehurst League in 1926, 1927, 1928, 1929 and 1930.

Proud Ticehurst cricketers having just won the East Sussex Schools Shield in 1946. Cricket in the village is documented back to 1888, when the Bell Field was the venue, but its best years were from the creation of the Institute Field in 1900 up to the 1950s. Back row, left to right: P. Rummery, M. Creasey, B. Bowers (Headmaster), R. Field, J. Olive, Mr Meacher, -?-, -?-, J. Fuller. Middle row: ? Pantry, L. Standen, R. Wall, C. Gardner, -?-. Front row: D. Crouch, P. Hayler.

'Welcome Home' festivities in Wadhurst for survivors of the First World War, August 1919. The location is the cricket field. 'Sticking the Ham' left to right are W.H. Newington, Owen Price, R.A. Gutsell, W.T. Bassett, H.C. Whitlock, Lt. E.A. Fazan and Sir George Courthope.

The oldest postwoman in Kent at the time. Pat Padgham delivers to Joan Weston at Rose Cottage, Lamberhurst, in 1940.

The old Chequers Inn at Lamberhurst has sat amidst cider orchards since pre-Conquest days. From about 1166 it was the Courthouse of the Manor of Lamberhurst, becoming a licensed coaching inn from about 1412. It has remained so, more or less, ever since.

A Hallford type C 2½T of around 1913 suffering a virtual write-off in the frontage of the Chequers Inn at Lamberhurst. To the Chequers it was less serious: it had been there since the twelfth century, and still is. Lamberhurst High Street nevertheless continues to present formidable risks to the careless driver.

Jack Oliver working at Beech House Press in Ticehurst. This old-established printing business had existed for over a century at the time of the photograph, being founded by William Balcombe in the 1860s. It then passed in the 1920s to Thomas Cooper and in the 1930s to W.P. Dengate. On the latter's death in 1942 Jack Oliver took the business on. The original site of the printing works was Beech House, behind the present butchers shop; when Jack Oliver took over, he moved it into Clare House on the other side of the post office (see page 52). A unique legacy survives from the earliest days of the business. To get paid for their contributions to the local press, Mr Balcombe and his successors kept a cut-out copy of all the columns of village news printed, to check that the price paid to them per line was correct. Many of these old cuttings books still survive, providing a fascinating record of Ticehurst events over many years.

Taking a break in the hop gardens at Foxhole Farm, Wadhurst, *c.* 1908. Front row, left to right: Montague Luxford, Eric Vidler. Back row: Will Hemsley and his sisters, with Mrs Hemsley.

Schoolday larks at Yeomans Farm, Wadhurst, *c.* 1912. Left: C. Wright. Upside down: B. Watts. Centre, kneeling: -?-, -?-, -?-, -?-, - ?-. Right, standing: C. Anscombe. Far right: H. Wright, -?-, W. Baldwin.

The château-like façade of Bedgebury School, between Flimwell and Kilndown, *c*. 1950. Its air of calm conceals a past of longevity and incident. When Henry III's bowmen marched south along the nearby highway to the Battle of Lewes in 1264, Bedgebury had already existed (as *Begcgebyra*) for four-and-a-half centuries. Queen Elizabeth slept here when on a 'progress' through Kent in 1573. She stayed to bestow a knighthood on Antony Colepepper, a member of a family that provided courtiers for, successively, all the Tudor monarchs and some of the Stuarts. The later occupancy by the Hayes family saw Sir James Hayes ('a mighty brisk blade', in the words of Samuel Pepys) use treasure acquired from his High Seas activities to rebuild the old house as a red brick 'Queen Anne' style mansion. The building was again greatly altered around 1836, when the new owner, Lord Beresford-Hope, literally encased the Hayes house in stone and added a wing at each end. The Beresford-Hopes were great benefactors to the locality, founding the Kilndown School and initiating the building of the church. Another consequence of their patronage was that in 1869 the old White Hart Inn at Kilndown was renamed The Globe and Rainbow, commemorating the Beresford-Hope arms: a broken terrestrial globe with a rainbow above it, inscribed with the motto, *At spes infracta* ('Yet Hope is unbroken'). The house became a school following its sale to the Crown in 1919 by the then owner, Isaac Lewis. The Crown retained the lands for forestry (they later became Kew Gardens' Pinetum), and sold the house to the Church Education Corporation to establish a school for girls. It opened as such in January 1920, and today it is one of the best girls' schools in the country. A wonderful internal feature of the school is the twenty-five foot square ceiling in the entrance hall, executed in intarsia and dated 1865. Produced by the estate workshops, and probably the finest work of its kind in the country, the ceiling is complemented by a set of striking marquetry panels in Kilndown church. They were rediscovered by accident in Cambridge in 1975.

The handsome gates to the Bedgebury Estate, prior to 1914. They were sited some 100 yd south of the existing Royal Oak public house, near the old Flimwell turnpike tollgate. Today some of the original gate lodges still exist, next to an A21 layby, but the gates themselves are long gone. A close study of the ironwork detail, shown in the photograph at the bottom of the gates, reveals that the central motif was the 'globe and rainbow' of the Beresford-Hope arms. A further supporter of the arms surmounts the gate piers, namely: 'In a crest coronet, a dragon, on spear transfixed.'

Wadhurst station in its South Eastern and Central Railway (SECR) days, hosting a special outing, probably a Sunday school excursion to London, *c.* 1910.

The old Rotherfield and Mark Cross station, in the early 1920s. One of the ubiquitous Stroudley 0-4-2T locomotives awaits the guard's signal to leave. The last train left the station for ever in June 1965, when it was closed; it had first opened on 1 September 1880.

A permanent-way gang working just outside Wadhurst station, *c.* 1920. Clearing embankments of overgrown woodland was, and remains, a task of 'Forth Bridge' proportions along all the Wealden railway lines. Overseeing the work is the Permanent Way Inspector, in bowler hat and suit. Sitting in the front row, smoking his pipe, is (probably) Charlie Parks, while 'Punch' Reeves is thought to be shouldering the pickaxe.

Wadhurst station in 1912. Designed by William Tress, built in 1851, and representative of several of his stations on the old SECR network, Wadhurst probably appears to be an unremarkable period piece today. But in its design a centuries-long pedigree is discernible. Tress used the architectural details first set out by the Italian architect Andrea Palladio in the 1500's. Today, anyone travelling west from Venice will see the Lombardy scenery dotted with 'Palladian' villas. Wadhurst station is a Palladian architectural fragment – a dolls' house version of the great Vicenza mansions.

The old Railway Tavern at Wadhurst, *c.* 1900, with proprietor A. Gibb at the door. Built not long after the station it once faced, its architectural detailing perfectly complemented Tress's Italianate station building. The Tavern was replaced by the present Rock Robin Inn in the 1930s.

Wadhurst station in 1875. A point of unusual interest is the dark line crossing the tracks between the platform ends. It is not a wooden footway for crossing the line, but a traversing line. Before motorized transport replaced horse-drawn vehicles, the latter were carried by train over distances too long to drive. A loading bay is enclosed by white fencing, just visible below the signal post; this was where carriages for rail transit arrived. Just out of sight is the turntable on which a flatbed rail truck would be loaded with a carriage. The turntable would then be swung through 90 degrees and the truck pushed across the main line, on the visible traversing rails, to another turntable at the end of the other platform. This fed a siding on which the carriage-laden flatbed waited to be affixed to its appropriate train. Carriages arriving at Wadhurst by rail were decanted by the above procedure, operated in reverse. The traverse rail process (a forerunner of the modern 'Motorail', according to railway expert Herbert Bassett) is the reason why staggered platforms exist on many rural Sussex stations. In Hastings Museum there are some excellent photographs of carriages loaded on flatbed trucks.

The journey necessary from most High Wealden villages before the railway could be reached, *c.* 1921. Although it was built on as high a level as engineering techniques of the day could achieve, the Hastings line still ran a mile or more away from most of the villages it served in this locality.

A quiet afternoon at the old Castle Inn, near Wadhurst station, in the 1920s. The inn had been there since the 1880s. It was preceded by the colourfully named Fox-in-the-Wood, located at nearby Spike Island. The Castle closed in 1971, but was reopened later as The Four Keys, a name it retains today. The white pipes visible at the station are part of a petrol gas unit which lit it until 1945.

Tunnel House in the early 1900s. This Wadhurst building was first associated with the nearby railway tunnel during its construction in the 1850s. The navvies used to lodge in the building which, as a result, became known as The Tunnel Hotel. The name is still discernible on the front in the photograph. Thomas Casterton, Wadhurst's postmaster from 1888 to 1910, was the son of one of the navvies.

Heathfield and Cross in Hand station, from the vantage point of the old tunnel parapet. Built by T.H. Myres in 1880, and seen here not long after, the station handled large amounts of agricultural goods traffic, particularly milk. From here the line ran on to Mayfield, then to Rotherfield and Mark Cross (see page 110). Heathfield and Cross in

Hand achieved national fame in 1895, when the country's first natural gas source was found just outside the tunnel. It was utilized to light the station until 1934, when the supply expired. The station was closed down in the 1960s.

Another William Tress station: Ticehurst Road, pictured *c.* 1920. Originally built in 1850 as Witherenden, the name changed to Ticehurst Road in December 1851, and finally to Stonegate in June 1947. A Stroudley D Class 0-4-2T is seen surmounting the up-line gradient to reach one of the highest railway summits (350 ft) in southern England at Wadhurst, four miles on.

A Cheesman & Newington coal dray, collecting from their coal wharf at Wadhurst station, *c.* 1910. Standing in the bowler hat is F.W. Griffin and, holding the horse, 'Brusher' Hayward.

Leading Wadhurst businessman Obadiah Thomas Corke in the 1920s. Born at Rotherfield in 1846, he moved to Wadhurst and quickly built up the leading grocery and drapery business in the locality. His principal properties were in St James's Square, Wadhurst (occupied today by the National Westminster Bank and Victoria Wine). Before selling his grocers shop to the bank in 1923, Corke had acted from it as an agent for the London County & Westminster Banking Co. Corke Estate Properties had interests in many Wadhurst High Street premises. Corke was also a Director of Cheesman & Newingtons, and in that capacity gave free use of one of their fields – Mr Cheesman's Field – to Wadhurst Cricket Club. A JP and a parish councillor for many years, Corke presided over at least four murder cases at Mark Cross Sessions. He died on 29 August 1929, leaving two daughters and one son, Harry Corke, who continued all his father's interests.

Youngsters of 1909 parade their cricketing talents. Among them are future county players (and one cabinet minister)! Back row, left to right: W. Cornford, R. Russell, R. Baldock, R. Weekes, F. Buffard, H. Stone, A. Sherwood, P. Hume. Middle row: H. Russell, H. Perry, K. Perry, G. Gasson, R. Cornford, C. Monk, L. Cornford, F. Packenham, H. Garner, E. Sawyers, C. Rummery. Front row: R. Johnson, A. Button, R. Russell, L. Garner, L. Croft, D. Blinks, H. Sawyers. Hurst Green cricket is recorded as far back as 1775.

Manor Cottages, Lamberhurst, bedecked for the coronation of King Edward VII, 5 July 1902. Edward, when Prince of Wales, was a fairly frequent visitor to this locality, notably to Bayham Abbey, Pashley at Ticehurst, and Wadhurst Hall – ostensibly on 'private' visits.

A lightning strike on 2 May 1921 destroyed one of the lowest lying houses in Ticehurst, at Lower Platts (above). Usually the church on the highest point suffered. On the reverse of this card the writer reports: 'There were eleven people in the two houses. Mrs Hodgson only injury 5 stitches from flying debris. She's the shoemaker's wife, all their belongings splintered to matchwood.'

This ten-pound aggregation of hailstones fell during a thunderstorm at Wadhurst on 4 June 1908. The photograph was taken thirty-nine hours after the storm. How it stayed so intact in mid June is a mystery; refrigeration was not that advanced in 1908!

Storm damage at Court Lodge Farm, Lamberhurst, *c.* 1887. Nearly a score of dead sheep lie under the oak they chose as safe haven from the storm. The size of the striken oak's girth is testimony to the awesome power of the lethal lightning bolt that accounted for both tree and sheep, a power in excess of 20,000 amps. Flashing between earth and cloud at 186,000 miles per second, the current discharge ('lightning'), heats the air it passes through to some 15,000°C. This causes violent air expansion, a sound wave ('thunder'), and converts any moisture encountered instantly to high-pressure steam. Thus, the moisture contained in the Court Lodge oak literally blew the tree apart as the electrical power condensed it to steam. The wet sheep ensured a perfect earth for the discharge; their internal organs would have resembled the tree damage.

Tidebrook church, between Wadhurst and Mayfield. It has nestled in its secluded woody dell since 1856, being built on land given by Joseph Newington. For all its isolation it still has a dedicated congregation who find their way to it each Sunday by many and varied means. The last war visited Tidebrook in several ways, including the encampment of several hundred Canadians in the surrounding countryside. They packed the little church each Sunday for the service. Another military man who found a final resting-place there was Hans Wagner, a crew member of a German bomber that crashed in the grounds of Wadhurst Hall in 1940. The lychgate is a war memorial to those of Tidebrook who fell for their country's cause.

Winter in Burwash High Street, in the 1930s. H.L. Petry's bakers shop is to the extreme right. On the pavement in front is a mounting block, a relic from the days of horsed traffic.

A Wealden snow scene with an anonymous shepherd, possibly in the Lamberhurst locality, *c.* 1910. The demanding lifestyle of the Weald and Downland shepherd was quite apart from other Sussex life. The writer Barclay Wills captured all aspects of it; his work can be studied in the recent book *Barclay Wills' The Downland Shepherds* (published by Alan Sutton).

Wadhurst High Street (*c.* 1905) in the sun (below), and five years later in the snow. The large building to the right is the Institute. The fir trees and railings next to it border the old village bowling green. Considerable discontent was caused in 1922 when the decision was taken to build the Commemoration Hall on the bowling green site. Many wanted the amenity to be kept and the hall built elsewhere. Higher authority prevailed, and the village was without a bowling green until October 1933 when C.B. Mould, F. Ratcliff and W. Grinham initiated the laying of the present one. It was opened by Lord Courthope in June 1934.

Arches erected in Ticehurst for a wedding, 1877. To the left is Edmund Newington's general shop; outside, holding hands with them, is Sarah Funnell, nurse to Dr Taylor's two daughters. Stephen Pattenden, Verger, Sexton and Clerk, stands in front, to the right of the arch; he died in 1918, but his son Albert (facing page) continued the tradition.

The same event, looking into Wadhurst. To the left is Lester's boot shop; opposite (right) is Mr Field's tailors shop. Mr A.E. Corke the chemist is standing to the right. The tradition of triumphal arches was a popular one in Sussex and Kent villages in pre-motor traffic days. Its origins are royal, going back to the arched reception route created for King James I in London in 1603.

Albert Harry Pattenden, Verger, Sexton and Clerk to Ticehurst parish church, in 1920 (left) and some thirty years on (right).

St Mark's church at Mark Cross. The church has perched on its little knoll since 1851, but for the first twenty-two years of its life it was the village school, built by Henry Dixon of Frankham. As such it was called Frankham Church of England School. During 1872–3 its conversion into a church occurred; a new range of school classrooms was erected behind it and re-christened the Mark Cross Church of England Primary School. Still there today, the school boasts a remarkable continuity of governorship; a member of the local Walter family has held a post on the School Board since 1851. The carved hymnboard inside the church is by the famous Frant woodcarver, Frank Rosier.

'A snow plough clearing a road at Wadhurst, Sussex.'

'Recalling the joys of their youth – two of the oldest inhabitants of Wadhurst enjoy a snowballing match.' The two delightful Wadhurst scenes on this page were discovered by the compiler in the Mirror Group Archives. Dated 10 February 1930, they have been included both for their picturesque charm, and so that Wadhurst folk can try to identify the persons and places in them. The original *Daily Mirror* captions are given, but offer no clues on either count.

Miss Caroline Foley, daughter of Revd John Foley, Vicar of Wadhurst (1846–86). Miss Foley initiated the village's interest in its history by giving a lecture in 1894. This was reprinted in 1923 by another villager, A.A. Wace, who used it as an introduction to the first published history of Wadhurst. The lecture was a kind of 'going away' present to the village, because later in 1894 Miss Foley married Dr T.W. Rhys-Davids, Professor of Pali and Buddhist Literature, London University, and Secretary of the Royal Asiatic Society. She became totally absorbed in Orientalism and an esteemed translator of Eastern texts. On her death Mrs Rhys-Davids left to the Department of Oriental Studies at Cambridge University an extensive and unique archive of such texts, together with a series of correspondence relating to Wadhurst local history.

Flimwell School before (above) and after (below) a flying bomb explosion in 1944. The school had existed since 1847 but was never rebuilt, its pupils being transferred to Ticehurst School. What remained stood derelict until 1980, when it was converted into a private dwelling.

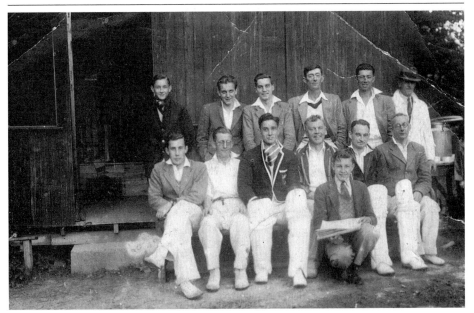

Flimwell cricketers on their ground at Seacox Heath, *c.* 1940. Not all identities are known, but in the front row (third left) is Hastings Pitman, and in the back row (left) his brother Robert. Both were highly competent cricketers; Ray Barfoot recalls seeing Hastings score 166 in 75 minutes. Both brothers were killed in the Second World War. They shared a notable father in Charles Pitman, who won eighteen rugby caps for England at wing forward. He also captained Blackheath Club, and played for Kent.

Flimwell cricket pavilion, shattered by the blast of a VI rocket in 1944. At the time the ground was located on the old Seacox Heath Estate of Lord Goschen. After this land was purchased by the Russian Trade Delegation in 1948, the Flimwell cricketers crossed to the other side of the A21, to occupy their present ground in the village.

The Annual Sports Day on the cricket field at Wadhurst, *c.* 1910. Winning the Pole Pillow Fight atop the Pole is 'Pitchy' Manktelow; losing it is Percy Lavender. W.H. Newington is judging, with H.C. Bocking (extreme right).

Wadhurst footballers in 1909. Formed in 1884, Wadhurst Football Club has always been a force to reckon with, not many seasons passing without an addition to their silver collection. Standing, left to right: C. Cogger, B. Cheesman, F. Skinner, J. Maryan, D. Cooper (Referee). Middle row: F. Turner, S. Clark, 'Pitchy' Manktelow. Front row: 'Babe' Dunmall, H. Watts, A. Palmer, P. Benge, F. Pattenden.

One of the SSZ (Submarine Scout Zero) class of airships passing over Flimwell High Street, *c.* 1916. Used for spotting German submarines trying to slip through the Channel, these airships operated locally out of their custom-built base just south of Polegate village. Nicknamed 'Silver Queen' or 'Silver King', they operated with much success until 1919, when the base was closed down; it was subsequently converted into the housing estate now lying between Willingdon and Polegate. (Another of these airships appears on page 47 in the *Around Heathfield* volume of this series.)

A ladies cricket XI with their male counterparts, probably at Lamberhurst, *c.* 1900. The photograph may show a wedding reception, but the men seem casually dressed for such an occasion. Nevertheless, the lady (seated, centre) seems definitely to be applying a googly grip to that ball in her hand, and the groom (?) looks very apprehensive!

The Mount at Wadhurst in the early 1900s. Seen rising in splendid isolation from a seemingly unbroken expanse of surrounding woodland, it evokes some Transylvanian castle. Still there today, it is in fact within comfortable walking distance of the village. Originally built by an Italian-based religious sect around 1880, it survives today as a notably successful school for handicapped children.

The bonfire to mark the coronation of Edward VII, built in July 1902 at Best Beech Hill, outside Wadhurst. The man on top is unknown. Next down, left to right, are: R. White, Mr Swift, C.A. Luck. Next down: B. Bacon, G. Tulley, F. Austen, -?-, -?-, -?-, A. Newington. On the ground: -?-, Mr Skinner, -?-, Mr Hyland. Bonfire and beacon burning has been a Weald and Downland skill for some twenty centuries; the high points of the Downs being utilized for signal fires against invaders, and ceremonial ones for the repelling of the same. Bonfire societies are still numerous and well subscribed to.

Wellington Place, Sparrows Green, Wadhurst, in 1905. Henry Deeprose's long-established grocery store and fishmongers is on the left.

Lexden House School Cousley Wood Wadhurst

Lexden House School, *c.* 1900. Not accounted for on any official register of teaching establishments, it seems to have had a quiet and private existence out in the Cousley Wood fields, off Monks Lane. What was taught is not now known, but the school (later Monks House) occupied an imposing Victorian sandstone villa, typical of many in the High Wealden area.

Albert 'Wiggy' Knight, Assistant Master of Wadhurst Boys' School, *c.* 1890. He was also Church Organist and Choirmaster.

Miss Hannah Watson at The Lodge, October 1904. Schoolmistress to the National Girls' School, Wadhurst, for nearly forty years from around 1885 onwards, Miss Watson was never seen without her hat. The Youth Centre today utilizes the old school premises.

Two bowls teams, one probably from Lamberhurst, in 1909. The Lamberhurst Bowls Club was established in 1901 and used to play on the green behind The George and Dragon provided by proprietor Mr Dale. Other local teams existed, too, including one at the Brewery. Perhaps it was they who took on a team from Tunbridge Wells in May, 1909. The press report does not give a score. Instead it quotes the verse:

> *Breathe not a word; too painful is the story,*
> *The brewers' hearts are sorry, sad and sore.*
> *Alack! Alas! for beer's departed glory.*
> *The blast of brazen trumpets sounds no more.*

Was the Lamberhurst Bowls Team slaughtered by the one from Tunbridge Wells? And are they both seen here?

Bernhurst, Hurst Green, home to the Packenham family since 1821, in the early 1900s. The present Earl and Countess of Longford still reside there. The original house has been enlarged in several directions over the years. Work was mostly carried out by diplomat Sir Francis Packenham KCMG. A rare (for this locality) feature in the garden is a 'wavy wall', to keep out the prevailing wind. Normally found in the exposed East Anglian environment, the serpentine masonry of such walls offers improved stability in high winds.

The Earl of Longford's chauffeur proudly posing with the family limousine, a Crossley of *c.* 1908.

The Hon. Lady Caroline Packenham, pictured in the 1930s at Bernhurst, Hurst Green. Originally from Ireland, the daughter of the Hon. and Revd Henry Ward of Killinchy, Co. Down, Lady Packenham came to live in Hurst Green around 1905. Following the death of her husband, the Hon. Sir Francis Packenham KCMG shortly afterwards, she devoted much of her time to village affairs. In 1926 she gave the land on which Hurst Green Village Hall was built, and officially opened the building the following year. Back in Bernhurst she was an extremely active gardener, and members of the family clearly recall her still planting trees with a spade in her nineties. When not working in the garden, she spent hours sitting in it enjoying the view. It was never difficult to find where she was; next to her chair she always had an electric kettle for making tea, with a lead that stretched all the way back to the house. To find Lady Caroline, it was a case of 'follow the lead'. When found, she invariably had her cat, 'Lord Christopher', for company. Lady Caroline died in 1938 aged 96.

A letterheading for J. Bassett's business. The attention to detail in it is typical of the degree of diligence applied by the family to all aspects of their carriage-building enterprise. The carriage types are, clockwise from top left: Ralli-Cart, Body Brake, Brougham, Landau, Carrier's Delivery Van, Dog Cart.

A delivery disaster at Durgates, Wadhurst, *c.* 1920. It could not have occurred at a more opportune place, right outside old Bassett's Forge. The latter may have made the cart originally; it looks like one of those used by Cheesman & Newington to deliver coal locally from the station. The corner poles tacked on the cart are clear evidence that overloading caused the axle fracture. The horse was probably best pleased about the event, having probably just hauled the load up Station Hill.

Some of the workers outside the widley known Bassett forge and cart construction business at Durgates, Wadhurst, prior to the First World War. Left to right: E. Skinner, W. Watts, J. Bassett, -?-.

A polo tournament at Lord Camden's estate at Bayham, August 1893. Polo came to England around 1869, from the Indian Army. Bayham was the ground of the Sussex Club, founded in 1875. Three remarkable brothers, J. Peat, A.E. Peat and A. Peat, played in each Sussex team from 1880 to 1893, during which period the club won the national championship – the Hurlingham Champion Cup – eleven times. The tournament at Bayham was the last time the Peat brothers played before their retirement; thousands came to watch.

Worthies of Wadhurst Town Band in festival dress at a fund-raising fête, July 1930. Back row, left to right: -?-, Charles Tompsett, G. Till, F. Still, -?-, -?-, -?-. Fred Tompsett is kneeling behind the drum, and next to the right is G. Blackman. (The others in the front row are unknown.) The band was started in 1871, and as well as performing at many fund-raising events it also competed annually in southern counties band contests.

Displaying its well kept appearance, the old Baptist chapel at Shovers Green, between Wadhurst and Ticehurst. It was first erected in 1817. Notwithstanding he was one of the 'brethren', the builder, Henry Kemp, had endless problems getting paid the £310 he had laid out. The chapel minute book records him as 'manifesting his hostile spirit' and 'pouring contempt on the church'. A year later legal proceedings against the chapel secured his payment. Somewhat whimsically the minutes record: 'Brs Hooker and Worsley went to Maidstone and paid Mr Kemp's lawyer (Thus the Lord appeared for us and delivered us from the hands of our enemies.)' The most notable pastor was James Jones who, at his death in 1888, had been there forty-five years. His memorial stone is clearly visible in the photograph, next to his wife's. The chapel remained active and well attended right up to the 1970s, the last pastor being a Mr Honeysett of Tenterden. Today it has been converted into a private dwelling and restored to its former smartness.

Horsepower, actual and mechanical, outside Bartley Mill, *c.* 1890. At this time the watermill had been operated by W. Arnold & Sons since around 1844. (They sold it off in 1902.) The mill's origins are indistinct, but it is known to have provided flour for the nearby monastery at Bayham before the latter's closure around 1525. Following a period

of wartime closure, the mill was completely restored to working order and milling started again in 1987. It is now a flourishing business, as well as a highly interesting walk-around museum. The cars in the photograph are possibly both Benz.

A sketch of the variously named Ticehurst Union, Ticehurst Workhouse, or Furze House, dating from the 1880s. Built by Sampson Kempthorne and opened in 1836, the workhouse combined the care of the poor of eight adjoining parishes. The large building to the right is the 'Iron Church' for both staff and inmates; it was dedicated by the Bishop of Chichester on 7 August 1876.

Ticehurst Workhouse in the 1920s. The parish magazine records frequent 'treats' for the disadvantaged inmates, such as outings to London, special concerts and great festive meals at Christmas. The building's functional layout seems unknown today, and the compiler has looked in vain for views of its internal appearance. Perhaps a reader can help in this respect?

A 1950s view of Furze House, showing the extensive range of buildings associated with the old Workhouse. One of the principal administrators there in the early years was Miss Anne Hankey (see page 50). The estate was an important source of employment for a great number of local people until its demolition in the 1970s. The modern development at Bewl Bridge Close occupies the site today.

The solemn cortège of a Salvation Army funeral procession passing along Lower High Street, Wadhurst, c. 1911. The deceased is thought to have been a prominent local landowner, Samuel Fairbrother of Walland Farm. In the top hat, leading, is undertaker C.W. Ashby.

The Revd C.E. Ward, Vicar of Salehurst, taking a service *al fresco* for East End hop-pickers in the old Guinness Hop Gardens, September 1938. Frank Brett is playing the cornet. Care of the thousands of itinerant 'hoppers' who descended on the Wealden hop gardens each year was well organized by the Red Cross and the Salvation Army, who supplied food, elastoplast and alleluias. A pioneer was Father Richard Wilson of Stepney, who 'emigrated' down to Five Oak Green in 1910 and, in an old pub skittle alley, set up his 'Little Hoppers Hospital'. It lasted sixty years.

New House with its beautiful iron railings, *c.* 1917. They were a showpiece of locally wrought ironwork, perhaps from the Lamberhurst furnace. The railing has long gone, but the house remains, as Primmers at Woods Green. When historian and Somerset Herald William Courthope surveyed the locality in the 1830s, New House stood on land owned by the Marquess of Camden. Then the property encompassed some 160 acres, and was tenanted by one George Smith.

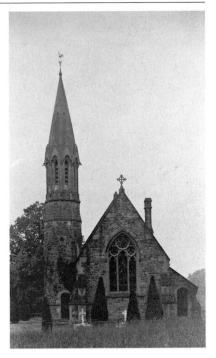

The charming little church of our Blessed Mary, in the grounds of Bayham Abbey. Dating from around 1872, it was built as a private chapel for Lord Camden's family and his estate workers. Popularly known as Bayham L'Église, it lasted about a century before being deconsecrated and converted into a private dwelling. The architect was David Brandon (1813–97), who built the nearby mansion for Lord Camden at the same time. Best known for his country houses in a style christened 'Jacobethan', Brandon also achieved notable prominence by compiling, printing and publishing at his own expense the Royal Institute of British Architects' first library catalogue in 1889.

Beechlands, at the bottom of Best Beech Hill near Wadhurst, c. 1913. This striking Victorian architectural confection was built by Edward Rayner in 1901 on the site of the very much older Skinners Farm.

Postmistress Johanna Francis (née A'Hern) outside her London Road, Hurst Green premises. Today it is a private house, but Miss A'Hern, who married Postmaster Mr Francis in 1933, worked there for over thirty years until 1969, nine years after her husband's retirement. When she retired, it was relocated to its existing premises.

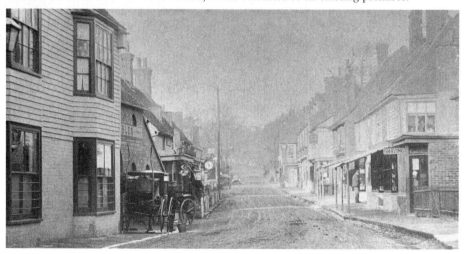

Wadhurst High Street, *c.* 1910 – waiting for something to happen! To the left is The Queen's Head, with its adjoining carriage yard. It was here on a summer's night in 1759 that Mayfield schoolmaster (and *bon viveur*) Walter Gale 'went with Master Freeman to the Queen's Head, where we had a quartern of brandy. I went to the supervisor's house and returned to the Queen's Head, and had three pints of fivepenny, between myself and three others; being invited to a mugg of beer we went into Mr Walter's.' Staggering home later, Mr Gale 'had the mischance of slipping from a high bank' and was told off by the Revd Downall for being drunk. Unperturbed, the indomitable Gale 'went into the town that night for more'.

Setting off for a drive from Walters Farm, Ticehurst, in the 1890s: a young Guy
Manwaring with his nurse. Farm foreman Daniel Leaney is the horse-holder. In a 1902
diptheria epidemic in the locality Leaney was to lose his wife Hannah, and their twins
James and Olive, aged 10.

Ticehurst in 1928. The picturesque frontages show little change from today.

A carnival outing on Lamberhurst Lea, *c.* 1909, re-creating the days of stagecoach travel. In fact most wheeled, horse-drawn passenger coaches avoided the Sussex countryside, using instead the few main roads linking London with the coast. One such ran through Lamberhurst. Anecdotes are numerous of coaches straying off the beaten tracks in Sussex and of passengers ending up walking after axle or wheel breakage. The delivery of mail, from the 1840s onwards, started to alter routings, but then the railways took over, making coach travel redundant.

The Faircrouch Lane Mission, or 'iron church' (above and below). As with all of its type, it was set in an isolated woodland clearing, well away from the nearest village, Wadhurst. A history deserves to be written of these unique corrugated 'iron churches' of Sussex, many of which, despite their deliberately remote sitings, still attract dedicated congregations. The Faircrouch one occupied this site from 1898 to 1946, having been moved from Woods Green. It was demolished in 1956. Incidentally, an 'iron church' was utilized to serve as Wadhurst Market Hall for most of this century.

A team of oxen doing their best on unyielding Wealden clay in the 1890s. The scene is no different from one which would have been commonplace in Saxon times, when the heavy clay plough (the *carruca*) was first introduced to the southern and eastern counties from The Netherlands. The one used in the photograph is little changed from the prototype. Illustrations in medieval illuminated manuscripts (e.g. the *Luttrell Psalter* of around 1335–40) show identical ox teams in use. There is much evidence, from Roman times onwards, that oxen (descended ultimately from the neolithic wild cattle *aurochsen*) were progressively bred for better draught capabilities, and for better meat. Hornless variants were bred to facilitate husbandry procedures in farms and markets. The longhorn variety persisted in the south, however, where oxen were often yoked to their load from the base of their horns. An ox had, on average, a ten-year working life before being sold on to the butcher. When the national population began to escalate in the seventeenth and eighteenth centuries – it doubled over a hundred years – oxen products (such as tallow for candles) were in great demand, and the London markets attracted the most business. Needing rich, lush pastures, the ox became an expensive animal to keep; the horse soon supplanted it, except for the heaviest work. It became common for several farms to have shares in the ownership of one ox team, each contributing to its upkeep in exchange for periodic usage. The last working oxen in Sussex were in use near Ditchling around 1938.

Wadhurst Church Lads Brigade in 1912. Standing, left to right: F. Goldsmith, C. Baker, S. Baldwin, G. Baker, C. Baldwin, Revd Hope, -?-, -?-, E. Grove, A. Collard. Front row: H. Ellis, W. Hubble, C. Ballard, P. Vince, C. Barrow. The Wadhurst branch was affiliated to the 4th Battalion Royal Sussex Regiment in the First World War.

The Court Lodge Gun preparing to join the Lamberhurst coronation procession, July 1902. The Morland family at Court Lodge had long-standing connections with the Indian Army, and mementoes of these days adorn the Lodge still; this gun, however, seems unlikely to have derived from such a military source, its bracing and breechwork seeming to owe more to the handyman's craft than the gunsmith's.

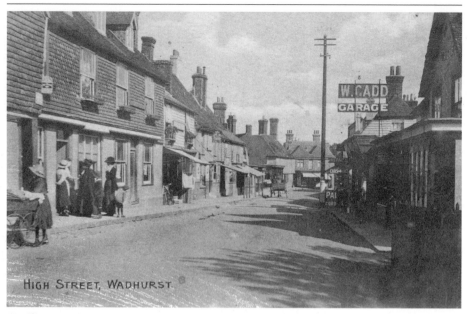

Wadhurst High Street, *c.* 1915 (above and below). Both photographs show that all men of working age were away at the First World War. The large building (below, slightly to the left) is the Baptist Chapel, built around 1866. It was converted into business premises in the 1930s.

The boys of Lamberhurst School, *c.* 1878. In their midst is their Headmaster for twenty-two years, Mr F.S. Jeffrey; other identities are not known. The distinctive feature of the photograph is the boys' dress. They are all hatted, one way or another; one (at the rear) is in a smock, while the rest are in a kind of Dickensian, 'Artful Dodger' rigout. A lot of them look the part, too! Most would probably have had only the one 'going to school and church' set of clothes, for their life outside school was largely agricultural, and miry. Lamberhurst School is seen at about the same date in the top picture on page 18.

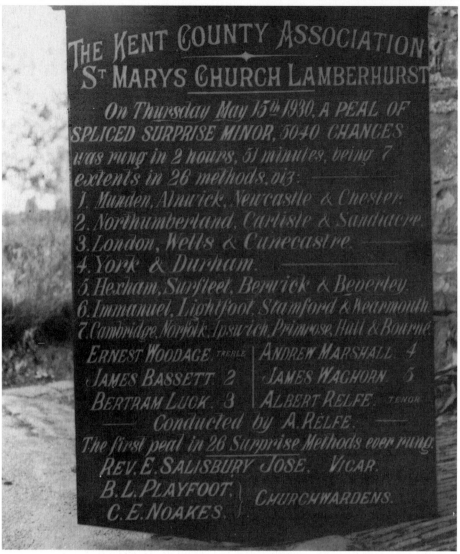

THE KENT COUNTY ASSOCIATION
ST MARYS CHURCH LAMBERHURST

On Thursday May 15th 1930, A PEAL OF
SPLICED SURPRISE MINOR, 5040 CHANGES
was rung in 2 hours, 51 minutes, being 7
extents in 26 methods. viz:
1. Munden, Alnwick, Newcastle & Chester.
2. Northumberland, Carlisle & Sandiacre.
3. London, Wells & Cunecastre.
4. York & Durham.
5. Hexham, Surfleet, Berwick & Beverley.
6. Immanuel, Lightfoot, Stamford & Wearmouth.
7. Cambridge, Norfolk, Ipswich, Primrose, Hull & Bourne.

ERNEST WOODAGE TREBLE | ANDREW MARSHALL 4
JAMES BASSETT 2 | JAMES WAGHORN 5
BERTRAM LUCK 3 | ALBERT RELFE TENOR
Conducted by A. RELFE.
The first peal in 26 Surprise Methods ever rung
REV. E. SALISBURY JOSE. VICAR.
B. L. PLAYFOOT.
C. E. NOAKES. CHURCHWARDENS.

A notable 'first'. It must have sounded wonderful, ringing out in Maytime across the hop gardens. The peal was constructed of seven basic elements – the 'extents'; each extent being a connected series of changes – the 'methods' named. Regardless of how many methods comprise the extent, each of the seven adds up to 720 rung changes, with no repetitions. Albert Relfe, conducting, would call the ringers to change into each method and, progressively, into each extent, thus 'splicing' the whole peal together. The joins should have been inaudible. That it was a 'Minor' peal means it was rung on six bells ('Minimus' is rung on four, 'Major' on eight). That the choice and sequence of changes chosen was novel, identifies the peal as 'Surprise'. Because local ability was quite limited in many villages, skilled ringing teams spent much time travelling to peal on little-used bells.

Salehurst's renowned ringing team, led by village policeman Albert Edwards. The serene and beautiful village church of St Mary's in Salehurst had a peal of eight bells, cast in 1771 by Pack & Chapman of London. A few originals still remain. The unique aspect of this peal (5,040 changes of Grandsire Triples) was that it was the first to be rung at Salehurst by an entirely local band of ringers – a rare achievement indeed in those days. Mr Edwards, second right, was a noted member of the elite ringers' Society of Royal Cumberland Youths. In a 64-year bell-ringing career, he rang 225 peals (mostly with the 'Youths') in 82 different towers, conducting 150 of them. His most complex was a Double Norwich C B Major.

One of the commonest rural sights until the First World War: the all-purpose general carrier, with his 'go anywhere' wagon.

A group of boys about to tackle the school garden at Lamberhurst, 1922. Back row, left to right: J. Redman, -?-, ? Drawbridge, G. Willett, C. Watson, Headmaster Mr Waters, J. Fuller, S. Parks, G. Davis (the donor of this photograph). Front row: K. Marshall, G. Arnold, R. Waters. Even in the Garden of England, Lamberhurst School garden was famous. Said His Majesty's Inspector of Schools in 1914: 'we have here one of the best gardens in the county, with vegetable plots, fruit quarters, flower borders, arches and beds.' The driving force behind its creation was the dedicated and instructional skill of Headmaster George Waters.

The Post Boy restaurant and filling station, a mile or so north of Flimwell on the Hastings Road, in the 1920s. Today only the house remains, somewhat less distinctive, and adjoined by a campsite.

The Tea Gardens at The Post Boy. The sender of the card, 'Will', writes that he left Sevenoaks at 11.30 a.m. and then 'stopped here for tea 3.30. Start for Hastings 4 oc. Lovely ride, weather splendid, plenty of cock pheasants by the roadside.' The date is 12 September 1922; what transport 'Will' was using is not recorded. Perhaps it was a bicycle.

Acknowledgements

The generosity of those who have loaned their valuable photographs for this book is gratefully acknowledged. Thanks are due especially to the following:

For Ticehurst: Mr A.J. Drew, whose initiative started the ball rolling; Nancy Gillham; Mr G. Fry for his invaluable help with Warrens Coaches; W. Sorrell; Nestor Nursing Homes for the Ticehurst House material; Glenda and John Kelvey-Brown of the Duke of York; J. Curtis; P. Oliver; East Sussex Record Office at Lewes for the use of the Ruth Collingridge Collection, and for extracts from the history of Hurst Green Iron Foundry; Mr and Mrs Holmwood of Battle; Mrs J. Buss of Bells Yew Green.

For Wadhurst: the Trustees of the Charles Bocking Collection; S. Cosham; C.J. Wilson of Heathfield; Mr H. Bassett of New Romney; Mr E.J. Hardcastle for use of the Courthope family archive; Mrs A. Griffin; P. Sanders; Mirror Group Newspapers.

For Flimwell: J. Scoones; R. Barfoot.

For Burwash: Mrs D. Pagden; Mrs R. Godfrey of Frogshole Farm, Biddenden; For Mark Cross: Mrs M. Walter.

For Lamberhurst: Mr and Mrs Uren, and the Committee of the Lamberhurst Local History Society; H. Haskell; G. Davis; M. Morland of Court Lodge.

For Hurst Green: Mrs A. Jenner, and the Committee of the Hurst Green Historical Society; the Earl and Countess of Longford, for access to the Packenham family archive at Bernhurst.

Lord Michael Pratt for use of the Marquess of Camden archive at Bayham; Mrs M.E.A. Kaye MA (Oxon), Headmistress, Mr A. Nipper, Archivist, Mrs Ryan, Librarian – all at Bedgebury School; Mr G. Batchelor of Kilndown; Gillian Price of the Harmer Family Association; and the Revd J. Lambourne, Vicar of St Mary's, Salehurst.

Interpretive help with photographic detail has come from many generous persons and institutions, principal among which have been the following: Dr J. Eisel of the Central Council of Church Bell Ringers, and the Macadam family of Barcombe, for initiating me into the world of change-ringing; John H. Moon of Lamberhurst for his encyclopaedic knowledge of his village; the Courier of Tunbridge Wells; the library staff of Crowborough, Tonbridge, and Tunbridge Wells; Chris Willis, Editor of *Ticehurst News and Views*; Bayham Trout Fishery; National Railway Museum at York; B.A. King, Librarian at the Rugby Football Union, Twickenham; Revd C.H. Atherstone, Rector of Frant; Annice Collett of the National Motor Museum, Beaulieu; Mrs D. Roy of Tidebrook; British Institute of Organ Studies; Fleet Air Arm Museum at Yeovilton; Tyrwhitt-Drake Museum of Carriages at Maidstone; Yorkshire Museum of Carriages and Horse Drawn Vehicles; Singer UK Ltd; Rare Breeds Survival Trust; Royal Institute of British Architects; Imperial War Museum; J. Oakley of Burwash.